The Order of Rome

Imperium Romanum

Charlemagne and the
Holy Roman Empire

The Rise and Fall of Empires

The Order of Rome

Imperium Romanum

Charlemagne and the Holy Roman Empire

Jack Holland, *Imperium Romanum*
John Monroe, *Charlemagne and the Holy Roman Empire*

Preface by M. Gwyn Morgan,
Professor of Classics and History
The University of Texas at Austin

CASSELL
LONDON

CASSELL LTD.
35 Red Lion Square, London WC1R 4SG
and at Sydney, Auckland, Toronto, Johannesburg,
an affiliate of
Macmillan Publishing Co., Inc.,
New York.

© Rizzoli Editore 1980

First published in Great Britain 1980

ISBN 0 304 30574 X

Printed in Italy

Authors: Jack Holland, John Monroe
Picture Researcher, Janet Adams
Assistant Picture Researcher, Noreen O'Gara

Historical Consultant, Judith Hanhisalo

Concept, Robert J. George
Design Implementation, Designworks

Rizzoli Editore

Authors of the Italian Edition
  Introduction: Professor Ovidio Dallera
  Imperial Rome: Dr. Flavio Conti
  Holy Roman Empire: Dr. Alfredo Bosisio
  Maps: Fernando Russo
Idea and Realization, Harry C. Lindinger
Graphic Design, Gerry Valsecchi
General Editorial Supervisor, Ovidio Dallera

Contents

Preface

Rome and the Romans still exercise a powerful hold on the popular imagination. Two questions arise time and again: How could the inhabitants of one small village on the banks of the Tiber River have conquered first Italy, then the entire Mediterranean world? And how could this empire, in some respects the greatest history has ever seen, have disintegrated as completely as it did?

However intriguing, these questions tend to obscure the significance of Rome's accomplishment. Rome's real achievement was neither winning nor losing territory but running an empire successfully for several centuries and, in the process, civilizing much of Europe. Without benefit of courses in business management or public administration, but rather on the basis of a certain innate pragmatism and tolerance, the Romans absorbed a world and governed it under law.

The Holy Roman Empire, which originated more than three hundred years after the fall of Rome, was a deliberate attempt to re-create in Europe the unity, the stability, and the culture of Rome under a new, Christian God. The ambitiousness of this attempt and the failure to achieve it become clear when we compare the two empires. The Roman Empire saw more than its share of civil wars and internecine strife but managed until its last days to hold together as a single unit. The Holy Roman Empire, by contrast, pursued the ideal of unity in vain. What was needed, but seldom achieved, was a balancing act between emperors, popes, barons, independent city-states, and dissident religious leaders—not to mention enemies beyond the frontiers. Far from unifying Europe under a single Christian ruler, the Holy Roman Empire remained a fragmented conglomeration, lasting as long as it did because it was weak, a counter in a power struggle played out on a larger board.

The same striking contrast between the two empires shows up in the cultural sphere. Putting Greek theories into practice (something the ancient Greeks often found difficult to do), the Romans regarded the city as the hallmark of their civilization and founded cities with all the appropriate physical amenities: temples, marketplaces, theaters, amphitheaters, circuses for chariot racing, aqueducts, sewers, public baths, even public latrines. In intellectual matters, however, Rome's highly cultured ruling classes left their subjects more or less to their own devices; the resources were there, but the aristocracy's concern was socialization rather than education.

In the case of the Holy Roman Empire, the theme of public building is practically exhausted once the castles and cathedrals have been described, but intellectual activity flourished. At first, education was rare even among the elite (Charlemagne himself, we are told, could read but not write) and so was sponsored enthusiastically by church and state alike. Later, the very disunity that plagued the empire encouraged the exchange of opinions by pen as well as by sword, spreading education through a wider segment of the population and leading to the foundation of the first universities. So Europe was readied for the influx of knowledge that came to the West after Constantinople fell to the Turks in 1453. And from Europe this knowledge, old and new, was spread still farther afield, to a certain rebellious colony where the Founding Fathers considered Roman practices a serviceable guide when they set about drafting a constitution for their infant republic.

In these respects the Roman Empire and the Holy Roman Empire resemble two sides of a single coin, both essential to the evolution of Western civilization but different in many ways. Yet the dissimilarities should not obscure underlying similarities, similarities of the human condition that tied these cultures to each other—and link them to us. In both worlds, the bulk of the population—peasants in the fields or workers in the towns—lived behind a veil of anonymity that is stripped away only occasionally by discoveries like those in Pompeii and Herculaneum. But we can still form a fair idea of what people sought, thought, and experienced by taking an attentive look at their history and cultural achievements. Their accomplishments reflect the hopes and aspirations of those distant times and yet speak directly to us across the intervening centuries. For these were people whose ideas and actions, wants and needs, all fed into the heritage that has made us what we are today.

M. GWYN MORGAN
Professor of Classics and History
The University of Texas at Austin

Imperium Romanum

Rome challenges and haunts the mind of Western man. On the one hand, it recalls images of the relentless drive to mastery, the thrill of triumph, and the dream of universal order. On the other, it confirms the unsettling ambiguity of imperialism as it inevitably succumbs to the malaise of decline. The sheer expanse of the territory Rome held under its sway has for centuries been a source of wonderment. By the beginning of the second century A.D., when Rome reached its greatest extent, the borders of the empire stretched from the Atlantic Ocean in the west to the Euphrates River in the east, from the vast African deserts in the south to the misty highlands of Britain and the thick German oak forests in the north. Altogether, the empire covered an area of about two million square miles, and its population totaled fifty million or more.

Upon the diverse peoples of the empire Rome im-

Fanciful legends were created to exalt Rome's beginnings. This Pompeian fresco (above left) depicts Mars, the god of war, and the royal princess Rhea Silvia, who bore the god twin sons, Romulus and Remus. The princess' uncle, the king, ordered the baby boys set afloat on the Tiber to drown (below left), but the river brought the twins safely to the city that Romulus was to found and give his name to. There a she-wolf suckled the two. This sculpture of the she-wolf (right) dates from Etruscan times. The twins were added during the Renaissance.

posed its legal system, culture, and language. Yet the empire was flexible enough to change and adapt as it absorbed. The Romans, however brutal, were not as a rule genocidal, nor did they attempt to construct a form of monolithic elitism—racial, cultural, or otherwise. Although no empire can be built on liberal principles, the Romans were never oblivious to the moral demands of the Roman good faith (*fides Romana*). From the earliest days, they were amenable to compromise, often enfranchising conquered peoples and bringing them into Roman society. By the second century A.D., the provinces were providing the capital with the emperors themselves.

The origins of Rome are enshrined in legends that have become part of Western culture. The best known tells how Rhea Silvia, the daughter of King Numitor of Alba, was made pregnant by Mars, the god of war, and gave birth to the twins Romulus and Remus. The twins' wicked granduncle Amulius, who had deposed Numitor, set the infants on the Tiber in a basket to drown. The river carried the twins safely, however, to the future site of Rome, where a she-wolf suckled them. Years later, after killing Amulius and restoring their grandfather Numitor to his throne, Romulus and Remus returned to the place where they were nursed by the she-wolf to found a city. The

legend tells that each brother chose a hilltop and waited for a sign from heaven. Remus saw six birds from the Aventine Hill, but Romulus counted twelve from the Palatine. Romulus thus built the city, gave it his name, and became its first king. Tradition dates the founding of the city to 753 B.C.

The origin of such tales can only be surmised. But archaeology has shown that the earliest settlers at the site of Rome lived not only on the Palatine but also on the Quirinal and Esquiline hills from about the tenth century B.C. Their forefathers were part of the great Indo-European migration that had begun over a millennium before and had populated western

Europe with, among others, the ancestral tribes of the Germans, the Italians, and the Celts.

Rome's site was a natural crossroads by water and land. Navigation from the sea up the Tiber ended at Rome, halted by shallows and an island; these barriers afforded the first natural crossing above the river mouth. Here, an ancient salt road from the sea intersected the north-south route between Etruria and the rich plains of Campania. The crossing was surrounded by steep and defensible bluffs and mesas—the so-called hills of Rome—that water had carved from the volcanic sediments of the plain.

The first settlers inhabited only the hilltops, leav-

ing the low ground for burial of their dead. These early inhabitants formed cults, joining with other Latin tribes that had settled in the region. One cult center was the Alban Mount, the volcano that had formed the plain. This religious unity eventually led to the establishment of the Latin League, over which Rome eventually gained hegemony. But in the early sixth century B.C., Rome fell under the domination of its Etruscan neighbors from the north, who transmitted Greek culture and instituted public works. The Forum, established at this time, served as a market and as a place for political assemblies, unifying the communities of the hills.

During the seventh and sixth centuries B.C., Rome was ruled by kings: Numa Pompilius, Tullus Hostilius, Ancus Marcius, Tarquinius Priscus, Servius Tullius, and Tarquinius Superbus (Tarquin the Haughty). The name Pompilius points to a mingling of Sabine neighbors with the Latin stock of Rome and Tarquinius and the dominion of the Etruscans from across the Tiber.

The Etruscans, unlike the Romans, did not speak an Indo-European language; legend and linguistic evidence associate them with the East. But both the Etruscans and the Italic tribes shared the Iron Age culture of central Italy and experienced Greek influence from the eighth century on. By that time, the

These black stones (top) near the heart of the Roman Forum marked, according to legend, the "tomb of Romulus." An archaic inscription found nearby contains the word "king." After the warrior-king Romulus, legend provided Rome with the priest-king Numa Pompilius, shown on this coin (immediately above) of the first century B.C. As Romulus was a military founder, so Numa was the founder of religious customs and the ways of peace. The so-called Walls of Servius (near right), credited to Rome's sixth king, made Rome by far the largest enclosed city in Italy and provide early evidence of work by Greek masters in Rome.

Etruscans had come to dominate the areas of Umbria and Tuscany and, in the late seventh century, parts of Latium and Campania. They also pushed north as far as the valley of the Po. In the sixth century, a Greek, one of many who had been assimilated in Etruria, established the Etruscan dynasty at Rome.

The legacy that the Etruscans left to Rome is incalculable. From them, for example, the Romans acquired the Greek alphabet. The Etruscan dynasty gave the city its first urban development, not only establishing the Forum but erecting the massive temple of Jupiter on the Capitoline Hill that symbolized the city's power. One tradition also relates that the sixth king, Servius Tullius, was Etruscan and that he gave the Romans their class structure.

This system was based on each citizen's ability to furnish certain necessities for military service. The richest class, the knights, was composed of those who could afford to furnish a horse and armor. Next in rank came those of moderate wealth, who were able to fit themselves out as heavily armed foot soldiers, with breastplate, shield, and spear. The poorest citi-

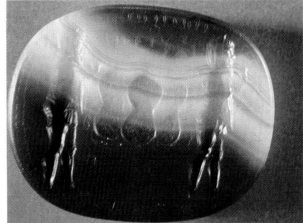

zens formed the auxiliaries, who were lightly equipped.

To carry out the assessment for military service, Servius instituted the so-called centuriate assembly, which met on the Field of Mars (Campus Martius) outside Rome. This assembly was later used for voting purposes and was organized to insure that the voting groups of the wealthy would always outweigh those of the poor. Servius is also said to have been responsible for dividing Rome into four tribes and for building its first fortification, the Walls of Servius, which made Rome the largest enclosed area in Italy, if not the world.

At the end of the sixth century, King Tarquin the Haughty was expelled from Rome. According to legend, his son had raped Lucretia, the wife of a noble. This outrage was the culmination of what came to be depicted as a classic tyranny in the Greek mold. For the Etruscans, the loss of Rome was followed by a series of setbacks from which they never really recovered. Having never coalesced to form a nation, they instead remained a loose association of highly individual states. In the end, this lack of national identity and institutions made them an easy target for the Romans, who seized the Etruscan cities one by one. By the end of the third century, the Etruscans were

The Etruscans were a major influence in Rome's development. Relics of their culture include this bronze statuette (far left) and this once richly plumed helmet (near left), with its elegant curled beard and curved horns. Above, the gate of Ferentino, one of the main cities of the Hernici, an Italic tribe that eventually was absorbed by Rome's expanding power. The helmet (right) of another Italic tribe, the Apuli, was decorated with a cross.

almost completely absorbed by their erstwhile Roman subjects.

After expelling its last king, Rome became a republic. In the new oligarchical constitution, the monarch was replaced by two consuls, who were elected annually by the centuriate assembly. Theirs was the *imperium,* or power of civil and military rule over the state. Other civil and religious offices gradually developed: praetor, dictator, quaestor, censor, pontifex, augur, aedile. Nevertheless, the consulship, the most powerful of the offices apart from dictatorship, remained the province of the founding families, the patricians, even after it was technically opened to a wider circle of the lower class, or plebs, in 367 B.C.

After the republican constitution came into effect, Rome scored a series of successes in asserting influence over its nearest neighbors. Expansion faltered briefly with the invasion of the Gauls, who sacked Rome in 387 B.C., but the young republic quickly showed recuperative powers. Within a generation, it had reestablished its position in Latium, reformed its army, and rebuilt its great ring of fortifying walls.

This was the age of the soldier-farmer, a time when, as the Greek antiquarian Plutarch was to write, "that pure and golden race of men was still in possession of the Forum." Self-possessed, frugal, self-sacrificing, and courageous, these men of Rome's semilegendary heroic age are typified by Cincinnatus. Summoned from his farm duties and appointed dictator in 458 B.C. to rescue a trapped Roman army, Cincinnatus

Below, a fourth-century B.C. tomb painting from Paestum showing a Samnite warrior. The Samnites, a fierce Italic people, aided Pyrrhus, king of Epirus (right) against Rome early in the third century B.C. The first to employ war elephants in Italy (below right), Pyrrhus terrified Rome's legions, but his wars were so costly that the "Pyrrhic victory" became proverbial.

simply performed the required task and returned to his plow. His story would be retold with bitter emphasis when the dictatorship later came to be abused as a tool of autocratic power.

From the Gallic invasion of the fourth century B.C. emerged one of Rome's first historical heroes—the general Camillus, who was credited with reforming the Roman army. Camillus succeeded in having the army abandon its old Greek-Etruscan phalanx for-

mation in favor of a more flexible organization. The legion was now drawn up in three lines instead of one, each line made up of smaller units, or maniples. Now that its army was more effective, the Roman Republic won most of the wars it fought during the next two centuries.

As Rome expanded, it adopted a flexible policy toward its closest neighbors and kinsmen, the Latin tribes. By 381 B.C., for instance, Rome had already granted citizens' rights to the conquered city of Tusculum. When most other Latin cities finally came under its sway in 338 B.C., Rome pursued this policy selectively, admitting some to full rights and others to the less-than-total "Latin rights." The cities in return were obligated to supply Rome with soldiers and to subordinate their foreign policy to Rome's.

Rome next reached beyond the Latins, south into the fertile plains of Campania and into central

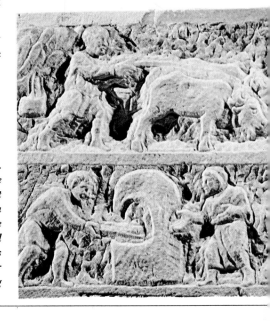

Of bread and circuses

Bread, like so much else at Rome, followed sharp divisions by class. There were three grades: "plebeian," which was black and was baked from barely sifted flour; "second," slightly refined; and "white," destined for the tables of the rich.

Bread was first made in Rome in the second century B.C., even though grains had been grown since the earliest times. Private ovens produced bread in the wealthier single-family homes, with bakeries serving the great numbers of apartment dwellers. On the march, the legionary carried an issue of wheat, which he ground with a hand mill and made into a rough whole-wheat bread.

Since grain was so vital to both the civilian and military diet and since Italy was not self-sufficient, the *annona*, or annual supply, came under public control by the third century B.C. From the end of the second century B.C., it caused persistent political strife. Grain for the poor was progressively subsidized until, finally, for the urban proletariat it was distributed free of charge. Only a bold leader could cut back these ancient welfare rolls.

The annona was a key to power—as well as a dangerous burden. When an opponent blockaded the grain shipments, popular discontent forced Augustus to launch a naval campaign (36 B.C.). Remembering this, Augustus kept the breadbasket, Egypt, as his private domain when he reorganized the empire. In a sense, the dole was a secret of imperial rule. As the satirist Juvenal wrote a century after Augustus: "The people, that once bestowed commands, consulships, legions, and all else now ... long eagerly for just two things: bread and circuses."

Above left, grain jars of the second century A.D. These great earthenware jars, sunk into the ground, were used to store wheat at Ostia, just south of Rome. By the mid-first century A.D., Ostia had become a thriving commercial hub and the main center for the shipment of oil, wine, and grain for the capital. The port boasted many mills (top center) and bakeries. This tomb relief (center right) shows a baker with a long paddle placing bread in an oven.

Bottom, the whole chain of the "annual supply," from tilling the field (top left, proceeding clockwise) to sowing, harvesting, threshing, transporting, milling, and finally baking in the characteristic domed oven. The baked bread itself appears in this Pompeian wall painting (right), with round, puffy loaves like some that have been discovered at Pompeii. The picture may have advertised the owner's trade, or perhaps the central figure is an official seeking popularity by distributing free bread.

Italy—an expansion motivated in part by the pressures of the class struggle at home. The plebeians, who were landless, could be placated with farms formed from territory won by conquest. For its part, the patrician upper class sought the prestige of command. As early as 396 B.C., when Rome destroyed the neighboring Etruscan town of Veii, thousands of citizens settled on the town's lands. This active colonization policy was to continue during the third century, spurred by the increasing political power of the plebeians and growing patrician ambitions. In 328 B.C., the Romans established a military colony at Fregellae, which commanded the inland route to Cam-

pania, in flagrant violation of a treaty. In 312 B.C., they built the Appian Way, the famous military road south through the lowlands and along the sea.

Expansion southward brought the Romans into conflict not only with the Italic Samnites but with the Greeks, who had been settling along the southern coasts since the eighth century. In 282 B.C., the Romans became embroiled in a conflict with the Greek colony of Tarentum, in southeastern Italy. Tarentum asked for assistance from Pyrrhus, the prince of Epirus in northwestern Greece and a relative of Alexander the Great. An able and ambitious commander, Pyrrhus landed in Italy in 280 B.C. with

Rome extended its dominion in Italy through the resilience of its citizen armies and the energy of consuls like C. Flaminius, who pushed the main road northeast to the Adriatic. The bridge at Rimini (above) was rebuilt by Augustus in A.D. 14. To the southeast, two other main roads met at Egnatia (above right); to the northwest, the great Aurelian road passed Libarna (below).

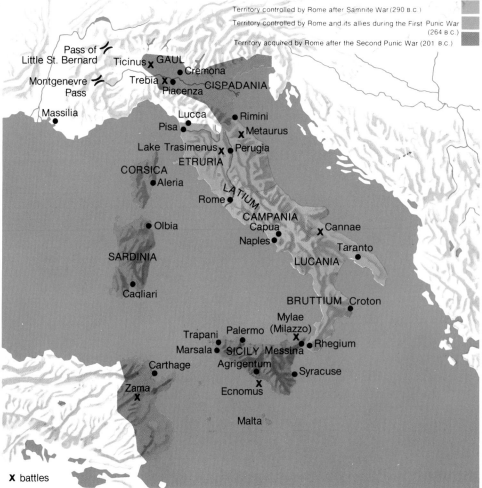

Territory controlled by Rome after Samnite War (290 B.C.)

Territory controlled by Rome and its allies during the First Punic War (264 B.C.)

Territory acquired by Rome after the Second Punic War (201 B.C.)

Pass of Little St. Bernard
Ticinus
GAUL
Cremona
Montgenevre Pass
Trebia
Piacenza
CISPADANIA
Massilia
Lucca
Rimini
Pisa
Metaurus
Lake Trasimenus
Perugia
ETRURIA
CORSICA
Aleria
LATIUM
Rome
CAMPANIA
Olbia
Capua
Cannae
Naples
Taranto
SARDINIA
LUCANIA
Cagliari
BRUTTIUM
Croton
Mylae (Milazzo)
Trapani
Palermo
Marsala
SICILY
Messina
Rhegium
Carthage
Agrigentum
Syracuse
Zama
Ecnomus
Malta

x battles

an army modeled on Alexander's phalanx system: Pike men, ranked twelve deep, were supported by a small cavalry force and a herd of twenty elephants. Pyrrhus' forces proved a formidable war instrument that took the Romans completely by surprise. In an initial engagement, the cavalry defeated the Romans, although it paid dearly for the victory.

Pyrrhus was so impressed with the Roman legions he had faced that he offered Rome a peace treaty, but his ambassador returned with a rejection. Another battle the following year also ended inconclusively. As the prince dryly remarked: "One more victory like this and we are lost." Pyrrhus decided to withdraw to Sicily. He made one more foray into Italy in 275 B.C. but was defeated at Maleventum. After this he left, never to return. On departing, he is said to have commented with ironic foresight: "O what a battlefield I am leaving for Carthage and Rome."

Rome was now a major city. The repulse of Pyrrhus had secured its position as the dominant power in central and southern Italy. Rome's most menacing new rival was Carthage, a city on the coast of North Africa. Founded by traders from Sidon and Tyre—the Phoenicians—Carthage was the heart of an emerging maritime empire. By the mid-third century,

A bas-relief (right) shows travel in a Gallic petorritum (four-wheeler) decorated in barbaric splendor. Although Rome created the first efficient road system, roads were designed primarily for military purposes. Shipping by land was almost prohibitively expensive. In the late empire, for example, carting wheat fifty miles could increase the price by one third to two fifths. Whenever possible, the Roman road (below) was built in a straight line, usually twenty feet wide. A surface of hard stone was laid over layers of stones in mortar, which in turn rested on a foundation of rubble. Below right, a chariot wheel. Because of the din and the danger, Julius Caesar banned all wheeled vehicles from city streets during certain hours.

The early guilds

In the days of Numa, Rome's second king, only eight craft guilds were at work in Rome: the flutists, goldsmiths, woodworkers, dyers, cobblers, tanners, potters, and coppersmiths. At the height of imperial power, the number had grown to more than 125. There were, of course, those engaged in the shipping and building trades: rope makers, caulkers, cabinet makers, brick makers, ironsmiths, and so on. Imperial Rome also demanded the services of barbers, tailors, itinerant scholars, poets, physicians, pimps, perfumers, and purveyors of rare fish, spices, silks, and pearls. Yet wealth did not generate large industry or mass production. Slave labor kept working rates low and free artisans often went unemployed. Burial inscriptions suggest that only ten percent of the artisans in Imperial Rome were of free birth. Many were freed men working under patronage of their former masters.

Reliefs from two sarcophagi: a cobbler working on a paneled cabinet (above left) and a woodworker plying his trade (above right). In Roman pottery shops (right), the most prized pottery came from Etruria, Greece, and Asia. In Augustan Rome the market in fine pottery was captured by the Etruscan town of Arretium, where most of the potters seem to have been slaves.

Various examples of commercial art from the thriving port of Ostia have survived intact. A shop sign (top right) offers poultry, rabbits, and vegetables as in any Mediterranean town today. On the counter are two monkeys—if not for sale, then perhaps to catch the eye. Behind the counter is a saleswoman, a common sight in ancient Rome. Although businesses and trades belonged for the most part to men, as the evidence of funerary inscription shows, women were employed in almost every type of retail selling and in the working of wool, which was traditionally a female domain. Often, especially among the lowest classes, women were forced to trade on their sex. This advertisement for a butcher (center right) shows the butcher with cleaver in hand. Cuts of meat—a head, a heart, and lungs—can be seen on a rack. Immediately below, a monument to two cutlers, with daggers, knives, and sickles on display.

Left, a stonecutter at work. In Rome, as in medieval cities, workers in the same craft tended to gather in the same street or quarter. Even though the competition represented by slave labor created widespread urban unemployment, cities swarmed with small artisans and vendors who made, repaired, and sold anything and everything. The working day in summer was about seven hours —in winter, about five. Immediately above, a bread and pastry shop.

Above, part of the entourage of a Roman magistrate: two trumpeters and lictors. Lictors, who were of lower-class origin, cleared a way through crowds and bore on their left shoulders the rods that served for punishment in early times.

the Carthaginians were established in Spain, Sardinia, and western Sicily, and their mercenary armies exacted tribute from the desert tribes of Africa. By 264 B.C., the distance between the spheres of influence of Carthage the sea power and Rome the land power had shrunk to the width of the narrow Strait of Messina, which separates Italy from Sicily. Once again, the immediate cause of the clash was a political initiative of the plebs, who voted to send two legions to help the little town of Messina ward off Carthaginian advances. Their success began a struggle that was to prove both long and debilitating, with consequences no one could have foreseen.

The First Punic War (264–241 B.C) began with a series of Roman victories, including, remarkably enough for a state of soldier-farmers, victories over the Carthaginian fleet. With characteristic pragmatism, the Romans devised grappling hooks to grab onto enemy ships, allowing the legionaries to board and clear the decks. In this way, sea battles became a kind of infantry engagement. These early successes were followed by disastrous setbacks, among them a defeat in a sea battle near Sicily in 249 B.C. But the Romans finally emerged victorious after crushing Carthage off western Sicily in 241 B.C. Rome promptly annexed the island, thus acquiring its first province. Loss of revenue led the mercenaries of Carthage to rebel, and Rome took the opportunity to annex Sardinia in 239 B.C.

The loss of so many territories made defeat all the more unsavory for Carthage and set the scene for the outbreak of a second and far graver war. The protagonist of the Second Punic War was Hannibal, one of history's great generals. Even two hundred years later, the Roman historian Livy would call the war "the most memorable ever waged" and speak of Hannibal as the stuff of legend: "Bold to the extreme in incurring peril, perfectly cool in its presence. No toil could weary his body or conquer his spirit. Heat and cold he bore with equal endurance; the cravings of nature, not the pleasure of the palate, determined the measure of his food and drink." At the age of twenty-six, this formidable leader took command of the Carthaginian army in Spain, where his father, Hamilcar, had been reestablishing Carthage's position after the losses of the First Punic War. Those defeats Hannibal was sworn to revenge.

Women

Women in Rome's founding myths serve essentially as means: Princesses were kept virgin for dynastic ends and the wives and daughters of the Sabines were unceremoniously snatched to give progeny and solace to Romulus' rough crew. Yet the Sabine women took the lead in arranging peace, and the queens of Rome emerge as equal if not superior to men: resolute, fierce, politically astute.

In ordinary life, males and females grew up together and were separated only at puberty. While the males studied military arts and grammar, the females learned how to administer a household. Marriage took place early and gave the woman considerable independence, although the male was master of the house and had power of life and death over the children. In time, women not only gained control over their own property but also over their own lives. This continued until the late empire, before Christianity changed the status of women. Matrimony then became recognized as a sacrament rather than a loose bond, abortion and infanticide were checked, and male supremacy grew. But Rome stands as the ancient society in which women played the most varied and active roles.

Above, a marriage ceremony of the oldest and most formal kind, restricted to patricians. The bride and groom sit on sheepskin spread over joined seats; they touch the ritual cake of spelt.

A literary education in Greek and Latin was available to women who could afford it (below).

The Roman girl required a dowry. Plautus' play The Pot of Gold *tells of a girl cursed with a stingy father. To help her, the lar (left), a god whose shrine appeared in every home, revealed a buried treasure: "The girl prays to me every day. She brings me wine, incense, flowers, and other gifts. For her piety, I'll reveal the gold."*

Immediately above, a midwife helping a woman give birth. The mortality rate in Rome was high. Early marriages and large families replenished Republican legions; in the empire, birthrates declined.

Hannibal soon found a pretext for launching his campaign. He captured Saguntum, a small town on the eastern coast of Spain that was a Roman ally, though within the Carthaginian sphere of influence. Shortly thereafter war was declared, and Hannibal disappeared across the Pyrenees with his army. Seven months later, in December 218 B.C., he emerged from the Alps into the valley of the Po, having completed one of the most extraordinary military feats of ancient times. Though the crossing of the Alps in winter had cost his army severe losses, it gave him the element of surprise—the Romans were caught with one of their armies on its way to Spain, and another in Sicily, preparing to invade Africa.

Hannibal assumed that he would be able to win the local Gallic tribes to his side when he appeared on the northern border of Italy. He knew that from 232 B.C. there had been trouble between these tribes and the Romans, who had annexed considerable land in the Po valley—under pressure, once again, from the plebs. Likewise, he hoped that by defeating the Romans in battle, he could win over their Italian allies, bringing about a collapse of Rome's support in Italy.

Hannibal, who spoke Greek fluently, had studied Hellenistic warfare closely. Above all, he knew the value of mobility. His first two encounters with the Roman legions, at Trebia (December 218 B.C.) and Lake Trasimene (spring 217 B.C.), showed that the Romans did not. On both occasions, the legions were outflanked and surrounded. In spite of these defeats they met Hannibal again, at Cannae on the Adriatic coast of Italy, in August 216 B.C. Though his army was inferior numerically, Hannibal was able to encircle and annihilate the Roman force by a spectacular outflanking maneuver.

Rome had suffered one of the worst defeats in its history, but the Romans reacted coolly. Varro, the general responsible for the decision to engage Hannibal in battle, was welcomed back to Rome by the people because, it was said, he "had not despaired of the commonwealth." Plutarch later wrote with awe about the Roman response to Cannae, amazed that a nation could show such fortitude at so great a loss.

In dire straits, the Romans made Quintus Fabius Maximus dictator and settled down to conduct a war of avoidance and attrition in Italy—a war of the sort the astute Fabius had advocated all along. The Romans had at last perceived that the war might well be won not in Italy, where some of their allies had deserted after Cannae, but in Spain, where the legions were more successful. Spain was an important source of mineral wealth for Carthage and a recruiting ground for its armies. Since Rome now controlled

Above, a Carthaginian coin depicting Tanit, a lunar and fertility goddess of North Africa that the Phoenicians, who settled Carthage, identified with their own god Baal. The coin's style shows how Greek arts influenced other Mediterranean peoples besides the Romans. Below, a soldier of Carthage. For the most part, the Punic armies comprised mercenaries recruited from Gaul, Spain, the Balearic Islands, and Africa. African cavalry was crucial to the successes of the greatest Punic general, Hannibal. Its absence at the battle of Zama (202 B.C.) gave Rome the victory in the Second Punic War.

When Rome expanded beyond Italy, a clash with Carthage became inevitable. As the most important sea power in the western Mediterranean, Carthage challenged Rome to learn to fight on sea as well as land (below center). Anchors and beaked prows from captured ships adorn the monument (below) to Rome's victory at Mylae (260 B.C.). Rome finally destroyed Carthage but later resettled the site with its own colony (left).

the sea, Spain was the only base from which Hannibal could expect supplies and reinforcments. Though Rome's forces at first suffered reverses in Spain under Publius Cornelius Scipio—a precocious young commander who was sent there in 210 B.C.— the Carthaginians were eventually expelled. A Carthaginian army did manage to slip past Scipio in an attempt to reinforce Hannibal, but it was annihilated before it could get to Italy. The news was vividly relayed to Hannibal, who was the recipient of the head of the defeated general—his brother.

Hannibal, meanwhile, had been frustrated by an enemy that would not stand and fight. Reduced to fighting inconclusive skirmishes, he was finally trapped in the heel of Italy. Scipio, on his return from Spain, determined to strike at Carthage by invading Africa. Despite opposition from the cautious Fabius,

whose defensive policy had kept Hannibal at bay for so long, Scipio landed northwest of Carthage in 204 B.C. Shortly aferward, Hannibal, after fifteen years in Italy, was forced to go back to defend his homeland. Ironically, the man he was about to engage in battle had gained his victories in Spain by using Hannibal's own tactics.

Scipio was not only a brilliant commander— "greater than Napoleon" one military historian has called him—but a Roman of a new breed. Steeped in Greek culture, unorthodox, impatient with traditional Roman attitudes, and something of a mystic, Scipio broke the rules that had previously applied to Roman generals. Not only was he young—he was only twenty-five when he went to Spain in 210 B.C.—but he was not even of consular rank, the usual prerequisite for assuming military command. In addition, he held supreme command for ten years, breaking the custom

Hannibal (above center) was remembered as Rome's most dangerous foe. He crossed the Pyrenees (far left) in August of 218 B.C. with about 50,000 infantrymen, 10,000 cavalrymen, and 37 elephants. He entered Italy by way of the Alps and annihilated the Roman forces in 216 at Cannae (above). Left, a war elephant. Scipio Africanus (below) neutralized Hannibal's elephants at Zama (202 B.C.) by leaving openings at invervals in his lines.

Left, a coin depicting a Roman galley. Above, a coin showing Romans voting in special saepta (pens). The political system emerged weakened from the Punic Wars. Below, Perseus, the last king of Macedon, who challenged the expansion of Roman power to the Greek east but was defeated in 168 B.C.

of annual replacement: No one before him had wielded such power.

In 202 B.C., the master met his pupil in battle at Zama, a town on the plains some five-day march from Carthage. Hannibal was deprived of his most important striking arm, the Numidian cavalry, which had joined the Romans. Disorder in the ranks of his army led to internal fighting at the height of the battle. At first, Hannibal's old guard stood by him, but, outflanked by the Numidian horsemen, the troops fled the field. The pupil had beaten the master, and the Second Punic War was over.

Rome was now the chief power in the western Mediterranean. Its next challenge came from the east. As early as 216 B.C., after Hannibal's massacre of the legions at Cannae, Philip V of Macedon had declared war on Rome. The Romans countered by brewing trouble on Philip's home front. A brief peace followed, but, with Carthage humbled, Rome turned toward Macedon on the pretext of championing several small Greek states that were protesting Macedonian aggression. After defeating the Macedonian phalanx at the battle of Cynoscephalae in 197 B.C., the Roman general Flamininus proclaimed the liberty of Greece, which had for over a century been under Macedonian sway. Flamininus—like Scipio an admirer of all things Greek—soon realized that it was easier to get involved in the internal affairs of Greece than it was to disengage. Subsequent quarrels among the Greeks soon brought the Romans into a war against the Greek king Antiochus of Syria. He was overthrown in 190 B.C. at the battle of Magnesia, Rome's first major conflict in the Near East.

Right, a fresco of Bacchus enthroned. The god of wine holds a cup in his right hand and a sacred wand tipped with a pine cone in his left. In the wake of conquest and increasing contact with Greece in the third and second centuries B.C., new cults were brought from the East. That of Bacchus, most of whose followers were women, brought orgiastic rites and spread disorders throughout Italy, with the result that the Senate voted a ban in 186 B.C. In this period Rome also imported the cult of the Great Mother from Phrygia. The priests of this cult castrated themselves; Roman citizens were forbidden to serve.

The Forum (preceding pages) was originally a meeting place and market for communities on the surrounding hills. It began to acquire civic functions and monuments under the last kings, becoming the center of the city and the empire.

Marius (far left) and Sulla (near left) first turned political rivalry into civil war, setting citizen armies against citizens and beginning the death agonies of the last century of the Republic. Below, a coin showing a triumphal chariot. Military victories became the springboard to political careers. Right, a temple near the Tiber port in Rome.

In 146 B.C., a die-hard aristocratic faction in Rome led by Cato the Elder found an excuse to go to war with Carthage for a third time, razing it to the ground and forming the province of Africa. The eastern Aegean seaboard subsequently became the province of Asia when King Attalus III bequeathed the kingdom of Pergamum to Rome. Rome was thus building an empire.

The Second Punic War and the wars that followed had momentous consequences for Roman society. During the exhausting struggle with Hannibal, the legions had been maintained in the field for fifteen years and more. Most of the soldiers were small farmers, whose farms fell into disuse. In addition, the conquests brought increasing numbers of slaves to Rome. Both developments tended to impoverish the Roman yeomanry, which had for so long carried the weight of Roman arms. Lacking both employment and land, the poor moved to urban areas in increasing numbers. Their anger grew as the landowners established great estates all over Italy and exploited them with slave labor. By the middle of the second century B.C., massive social upheaval was impending. When it finally came, it was precipitated by the growing power of the plebeian tribunes, officials who, since the fifth century B.C., had been elected annually to protect the legal rights of the poor. The tribunes became the spokesmen for the discontent that would inspire the so-called Roman Revolution, which would ultimately undermine the republic.

The most powerful of the tribunes were the brothers Gracchi, Tiberius and Gaius, relatives of the great Scipio. Their legislative proposals outraged the wealthy landowners. In 133 B.C., Tiberius proposed that the state-owned lands—which, though public,

were in fact left at the disposal of the rich—be divided up into small holdings. Though his legislation was passed, he was killed the same year in a riot between his supporters and a senatorial faction. In 122 B.C., Gaius tried to win the support of the urban proletarians by proposing that they receive an allowance of cheap grain. He also courted the increasingly influential commercial interests, particularly the tax collectors, by proposing that they be allowed five-year contracts to collect taxes in the recently acquired and very rich province of Asia. A hostile faction of the Senate clashed with his followers, and Gaius committed suicide when the fighting went against him. In the witch hunt that ensued, three thousand of his supporters were killed. Nevertheless, the Gracchi had ex-

Feasting as the Romans did

"Lucullan feasts," "dinners like Trimalchios'"—the culinary preferences of Rome's grandees, real and imaginary, have become proverbial. The menu might have included "a huge lobster, garnished with asparagus, . . . a mullet from Corsica, . . . the finest lamprey the Straits of Sicily can purvey, . . . a goose's liver, a capon as big as a house, a boar piping hot, . . . truffles and delicious mushrooms. . . ." Thus did the satirist Juvenal describe a banquet of the first century A.D.

Earlier Romans had been more frugal, proud of what they grew at home. Turnips were a national food and remained a favorite at all periods. The one main meal (cena) took place toward evening, although a glutton like the emperor Nero sat down for a cena at noon. The Romans ate while reclining on sloping couches arranged around a square table. Not having forks, they used their fingers in addition to spoons, ladles, and knives. A full-scale banquet might consist of at least seven courses: the hors d'oeuvres, three entrées, two roasts, and the dessert. Eggs and honey mixed with wine always opened the dinner, and wine mixed with water accompanied every course. The dessert included spicy foods meant to stimulate the desire for drink. There was a taste for imaginative dishes—one meat disguised to resemble another, game stuffed with game of different sorts, mushrooms steeped in honey, fish with pulped fruit. It was proper for guests to eat until about to burst, then to induce vomiting and start again.

Above left, Roman kitchen utensils made of bronze. Left, fish and squid. The Romans were fond of seafood of all kinds, much of which came from nearby areas of the Mediterranean. Oysters were especially prized, above all those from the eastern coast of Britain, near Colchester. Above, a Pompeian trompe l'oeil fresco showing pomegranates, apples, figs, and grapes in a realistic transparent glass bowl.

Left, a Pompeian fresco from the house of Julius Felix depicting a death scene from the third century B.C. Reclining on a sloping couch similar to the triclinium on which the wealthier Romans dined is the African princess Sophonisba. The princess was the daughter of Hasdrubal Gisgo and the wife of Syphax, an African ally of Carthage. After Syphax's defeat at the battle of the Great Plains in Africa in 204 B.C., she was captured by Rome's ally Masinissa, who fell in love with her and married her on the spot. The Romans, embarrassed by this, asked him to divorce her. Rather than comply, he sent her a cup of poison, which she drank—apparently, gladly. Below, a glass vessel from Imperial Rome, used for drinking wine.

Left, glass bottles from the Imperial period, when glass production was stimulated by a decline in the quality of pottery. After the Roman conquest of Egypt at the end of the first century B.C., glass was exported to Rome in ever-increasing quantities. This cup in thrown metal (above) from the Imperial age shows Odysseus addressing Philoctetes on the island of Lemnos.

Pompey, called the Great (above), made Syria a Roman province. Left, the central gate of Hierapolis in Syria. Pompey pushed almost to the Caspian Sea in pursuit of the Pontic king Mithridates. What kept him from reaching the Caspian, so the story goes, were swarms of serpents.

posed the deep divisions within Roman society, divisions that led to the rise of men like Gaius Marius and Julius Caesar, whose popular support would no longer rest on the votes of the plebs but on the swords of the legions. What these men learned from the fate of the Gracchi was that anyone who challenged the powerful conservative factions within the Senate could succeed only with an army at his back.

The century after the deaths of the Gracchi was dominated more by internal than by external wars. For the most part, these were fought between loose factions representing the two political tendencies: the *populares,* appealing more explicitly to broad popular support and championing the cause of the plebs; and the *optimates,* favoring older political customs and the historic, unquestioned leadership of the Senate. Gaius Marius, born the son of poor parents in 157 B.C., belonged by birth and inclination to the people's faction. He rose through the ranks of the army, became a tribune, and won the command of the legions in Africa against Jugurtha, a rebel prince. Jugurtha was finally bested, but only by the machinations of the man who became Marius' deadly enemy—Cornelius Sulla. Marius, however, won the adulation of Rome by defeating two armies of Germans who had been threatening Italy during the last years of the second

century B.C. In the process, he revolutionized the Roman army by drafting into it for the first time the very poor, without reference to property qualifications. He thus gave the Roman state the ambiguous benefit of a thoroughly professional army.

At the same time, Marius was elected to the consulship six times—a record. His rivals decided to make sure that this upstart was taught a lesson. When Marius attempted to reward his veterans with land grants, he was opposed by optimates in the Senate. In the violence that followed, a candidate for the consulship was killed by supporters of Marius, whose domination of politics in the city thus ended. Hoping to open new opportunities for himself in the East, he departed—angry, unforgiving, and bitter.

Marius was recalled to defend Rome once again during the so-called Social Wars, which were fought over Rome's policies toward its allies. Proposals to extend full citizenship to Rome's allies in Italy had been championed since the time of Gaius Gracchus. In 91 B.C., a tribune at Rome, Marcus Livius Drusus, was assassinated while pressing the Italian's case. His death sparked a fierce rebellion that was not brought under control until Rome granted the rights it had withheld. Old age and sickness kept Marius from playing an important role in the Social Wars and the glory went instead to Sulla, his archrival and the

Pompey's brilliant antagonist and conqueror was Julius Caesar (right), who claimed descent from Romulus himself. One of the most extraordinary men of all time, Caesar was a first-class orator, daring general, and consummate politician, as well as an accomplished prose writer, pamphleteer, and poet. His energy appeared boundless. While on his way to Spain during the Civil War, he composed a pamphlet, a poem describing his trip, and part of his famous account of the war. Though he pursued power indefatigably, the Roman biographer Suetonius says: "The resentment he entertained against anyone was never so implacable that he did not willingly renounce it when the chance came." Below, the Rubicon River. On January 11, 49 B.C., Caesar crossed the river into Italy, thus inviting the Civil War.

The Gallic Wars

First relentless war—then veterans owning land and settling in strong towns, a need for intermarriage, and the proliferation of trade and administrative ties between Rome and the provinces. In this way, Rome's expanding power brought acculturation. Most fateful for the shape of modern Europe were Julius Caesar's campaigns in Gaul. Caesar subdued the Belgae, Aquitanes, and Celts in the area from the Mediterranean to the English Channel, and from the Atlantic to to the Rhine. (He could not, however, establish an enduring presence across the Rhine, and the Germans were never Romanized.) On the pretext that migration by the Helvetii from Switzerland into Gaul threatened Rome's interests, Caesar moved in 58 B.C.

The following year, when campaigning against the Belgae in the north, he met with an ambush and near massacre of his legions. Characteristically, his own presence of mind and the discipline of his men eventually saved the day. Rome's expeditions across the Rhine and English Channel provoked the Gauls, who united in revolt against the Roman invaders. The leader of the resistance, Vercingetorix, was defeated at Alesia, where the French have commemorated his valor with a colossal statue that broods over the land. The vanquished chief was put on display in Rome and then strangled in a dungeon at the foot of the Capitoline Hill. Despite a spirited resistance, Gaul eventually succumbed to imperial discipline. In time, the land became Latinized, conserving and transmitting imperial values to the West.

Far left, a statue of Caesar the conqueror, believed to have been carved in his lifetime. This Roman view of Gaul (facing page, below right), with its walled towns, is from an eleventh-century copy of an imperial map that showed all military roads from Britain to the Euphrates. Above, a coin showing Vercingetorix, Caesar's vigorous but unlucky adversary. When Caesar was besieging him at Alesia, the Romans dug and held twenty-five miles of trenches.

Above center, a relief from the mausoleum of the Julii at St.-Rémy-de-Provence depicting a battle between the Romans and the Gauls. The ordinary Gallic warrior thought it unmanly to wear armor, apart from a helmet (below). Left, a Gallic prisoner. Many prisoners were displayed in chains when Caesar finally celebrated his triumph over the Gauls in 46 B.C. Romanization brought improved technology: right, a Roman bridge at Voison. Below right, a Roman helmet found near the battleground of Alesia.

Julius Caesar succumbed to the charms of Egypt's queen Cleopatra, as did his bluff lieutenant and military heir, Mark Antony (left). Not so Octavian, Caesar's great-nephew. When Octavian defeated Antony, Cleopatra committed suicide (above).

Senate's champion. As the wars neared their end, Sulla was given command of the eastern province of Asia, which had been invaded by Mithridates, the king of the Black Sea kingdom of Pontus. But before Sulla could leave, a tribune of the people's party transferred the command of the army to Marius. Sulla's response stunned Rome: He marched on the city.

Marius fled, abandoning his supporters, and for a year Rome's former savior led the life of a vagabond and criminal. When Sulla left in pursuit of Mithridates, however, Marius returned to Rome and entered his seventh consulship. He rode through the city streets, old, haggard, decrepit, and bent on revenge—which he quickly inflicted on those who had previously opposed him. Employing a gang of cutthroats, he murdered all those he even remotely suspected as threats. "When maimed and headless carcasses were now frequently thrown about and trampled upon the streets, people were not so much moved with compassion at the sight, as struck into a kind of horror and consternation," wrote Plutarch of the butchery. Finally, Sertorius, a member of the people's faction and a capable young general, moved against the gang and had them exterminated at night in their barracks. Shortly afterward, Marius died of natural causes. Rome heaved a sigh of relief—prematurely, as it turned out. Sulla was still to have his day.

By 81 B.C., Sulla was back in Rome, after defeating the forces of the people's faction throughout Italy and crushing an uprising of the Samnite tribes. On being elected dictator, he embarked on a purge of his opponents. First, he massacred six thousand Samnite prisoners in the circus. He was addressing the Senate nearby when the screams of the victims began to distract his listeners. Sulla told the Senators not to pay attention to the noise, that it was merely some "offenders being chastised." This done, Sulla drew up a list of one hundred Senators and one thousand knights and had these individuals executed on the pretext of their support for Marius. His real aim, as often as not, was to get his hands on the victims' wealth, which he confiscated and awarded to his henchmen. Sulla then set out to destroy the political power of the plebeian assembly and its tribunes. When he had finished his task, cold-bloodedly and thoroughly, he resigned his dictatorship and abandoned himself to a debauched life. He died shortly afterward. One hostile tradition had it that a vile disease left his body consumed by worms.

Sulla had checked the impetus of the people and restored the Senate to its former prominence. But this measure was merely a stopgap—the republican oligarchy was doomed. Two forces were now uniting to end it: the interests of the legions, which now enrolled the landless, and the ambitions of their generals. The stage was set for Pompey and Caesar.

When Sulla died, Caesar was still a young man, exiled because Marius had been his uncle by marriage. Other men—supporters of Sulla—were the

dominant leaders in Rome: Lucius Lucullus, Licinius Crassus (who had become enormously wealthy during the Sullan purges), and Gnaeus Pompey, the young general whom his troops had hailed as *Magnus,* "the Great." But Pompey's reputation as a soldier and commander owed less to actual performance than to flattery, to which he readily succumbed. A man of scant political judgment, Pompey was too easily manipulated.

Pompey's first important commission after the death of Sulla was to quell a rebellion of the people's faction led by Sertorius. After Marius' death, Sertorius had fled to Spain and organized Spanish tribesmen into a guerrilla army that had continually outsmarted the Roman armies sent against it. Pompey at first fared no better than the others before him, but he was eventually able to exhaust the Spanish tribes' willingness to fight as well as their loyalty to Sertorius. Sertorius was assassinated and his movement soon collapsed.

Pompey then returned to Italy just in time to take

part in crushing the slave revolt led by the gladiator Spartacus (73–71 B.C.). The uprising—the most serious of many in that period—had been brought under control by Crassus by the time Pompey finally arrived. Yet even reflected glory glittered: Pompey and Crassus were elected consuls for the year 70 B.C. Three years later, Pompey was voted extraordinary powers to suppress the pirates who reigned unchecked throughout the Mediterranean, a task he executed with great efficiency. Further glory was bestowed on him when he was sent to the East to relieve Lucullus, who had been fighting a drawn-out but successful campaign against the still active Mithridates.

In 62 B.C., having put Rome's presence in the East on a new, more solid footing, Pompey came back to Rome laden with spoils and evoking comparisons to Alexander the Great. In the meantime, the young Caesar had shown himself to be a brilliant demagogue. Imprudently disbanding his army, Pompey was forced to align himself with Caesar and Crassus—by now the wealthiest man in Rome—when

Octavian's victory at Actium ushered in a welcome period of peace. The Altar of Augustan Peace, decreed by the Senate, depicts leaders of the Senate and the family of Augustus (left), as well as Augustus' legendary ancestors Romulus and Aeneas. Augustus himself had commemorated his war on the assassins of Julius Caesar by building the great temple to Avenging Mars that dominated the new Forum in the heart of Rome (below left). This statue of Augustus (below), in heroic Greek attitude, is an idealized representation depicting the emperor as a god.

The expansion of the empire

Originally an insignificant town on the banks of the Tiber, Rome grew to become the center of one of the most powerful and vast empires the world has ever known. By the beginning of the second century A.D., the Roman Empire had reached its greatest extent, encompassing an enormous variety of peoples, cultures, and religions.

Through a series of wars and conquests, Rome gained more and more territory. The peak of this expansion occurred during the reign of Trajan. Under his rule, the province of Dacia, which stretched approximately from the lower Danube to the Black Sea, was brought under Roman sway. Trajan also created the provinces of Assyria and Mesopotamia after capturing the Parthian capital of Ctesiphon in A.D. 114. Administrative exigencies later forced the division of the empire into eastern and western sections.

Augustus

By force, political acumen, and administrative foresight, Augustus (below) turned the heritage of Julius Caesar into a monarchy that could endure. His Julio-Claudian dynasty failed to penetrate Germany but succeeded in annexing Britain.

The Flavians

Under the Flavians, the area between the upper Rhine and Danube was subdued and the Danube fortified.

The Antonines

The dynasty of the Antonines brought the empire of Rome to its peak. Under Trajan (A.D. 98–117) the empire reached its greatest extent, coming to embrace the provinces of Dacia, Arabia, Armenia, Mesopotamia, and Assyria. Trajan's successors generally followed a policy of retrenchment. With Commodus (below), the Antonine line ended.

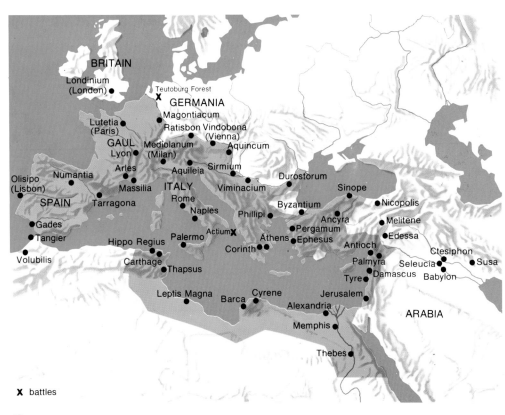

X battles

Conquests of Trajan

Commodus

The reign of Commodus, according to Gibbon, marked the beginning of the empire's decline and fall. Commodus' assassination was followed by a year of anarchy that ended when the first emperor from Africa, Septimius Severus (A.D. 193–211), came to the throne and founded the dynasty of the Severi. The imperial borders remained fairly static during this period, which produced no really able emperors apart from Septimius himself. He contested with several rivals for the throne and grappled with serious economic problems that were to plague the empire until its collapse. Because of the need to buy off his troops during the Civil War, Septimius depreciated the currency drastically. In the following decades, this practice led to chronic inflation and a weakening of the already ailing imperial economy. Septimius also faced recurrent troubles with the Parthians and in Britain. He was succeeded by his son Caracalla (A.D. 211–217), who inherited his father's inflationary practices. Like his father, Caracalla increased the legionaries' pay. His extravagant wars on the Danube forced a further devaluation of the currency. It was during his reign that Roman citizenship was extended to all people of the empire—making them liable to an inheritance tax. His successor was Elagabalus (below), a priest of the sun god Ela-Gabal in Syria who claimed to be Caracalla's bastard son. A transvestite, Elagabalus worshiped the sun god in the form of a black phallic meteorite. He attempted to introduce this bizarre cult in Rome but was assassinated. He was succeeded by his cousin, Alexander Severus (A.D. 222–235), a thirteen-year-old boy with whom the dynasty ended.

Constantine

The dynasty of Constantine (below) lasted nearly sixty years. By this time, the empire's borders had already begun to shrink. In A.D. 273, Dacia had been abandoned to the barbarians, who kept up unrelenting pressure on the empire for the next two centuries. Constantine made Christianity the official religion and moved the capital of the empire from Rome to a site on the Bosporus. Financing the new capital, Constantinople, further debilitated the already weakened imperial finances. Constantine was succeeded by his sons before his nephew Julian became sole emperor in A.D. 361. The most able of Constantine's successors, Julian had little time to exercise his abilities.

Flavius Honorius

The emperor Flavius Honorius (below) ruled in the Latin West of the empire (A.D. 393–423) as a nominal head of state. From the security of the marshes around Ravenna, Honorius watched Spain fall to the Vandals, Rome being sacked by the Goths, and Britain evacuated by the Romans: He could do nothing to stem the barbarian tide. Until A.D. 408, the German mercenery Stilicho had acted with vigor in the imperial cause, but he was murdered at the instigation of Honorius. When Honorius died in A.D. 423, his sister Galla Placidia ruled in the West through her infant son.

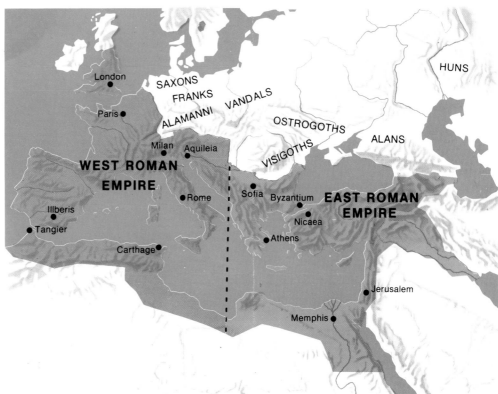

the Senate proved stubborn about ratifying his Eastern settlements and even balked at sanctioning land allotments to his veterans. On Caesar's initiative, Pompey and Crassus joined Caesar in a commission of three—the first triumvirate—to manage public affairs. They supported Caesar's candidacy for the consulship of 59 B.C. The consul in turn saw to it that Pompey's Eastern settlements were ratified and that the interests of the tax collectors, Crassus' friends, were protected. After his consulship ended, Caesar was given the governorship of Transalpine Gaul. Rome's great master thus gained command of the legions that in the not-too-distant future he would forge into the instrument of absolute rule.

In an age of exceptional men, Gaius Julius Caesar stood out. His family was patrician, although obscure in recent generations. But it proudly traced its line to Romulus and even to his heroic forebear, the legendary Trojan Aeneas, son of Venus. Many years before, Sulla had warned someone who scoffed at the young Caesar's apparent vanity and idleness: "That man contains many Mariuses." One of Rome's greatest modern historians, Theodor Mommsen, described him as "the perfect man." No one can contest Caesar's abilities as orator, politician, and general. Bold in strategy and tactics and incredibly quick in action,

Above, a bust of Marcus Vipsanius Agrippa. After the death of Julius Caesar, Agrippa—a man of obscure origins—had a profound effect on the fortunes of Octavian, who was Caesar's heir and the future emperor. An outstanding general, Agrippa successfully quelled an uprising in Gaul, crossed the Rhine, and resettled a Germanic tribe from Gaul—the Ubii—in Germany. When Octavian's control in Italy was threatened by a blockade of the grain supply, he routed the fleet of Pompey's son off the coast of Sicily. In addition, he organized and directed the final victory over Antony and Cleopatra at Actium. For the last ten years of his life, he became part of Augustus' dynastic schemes, fathering five children by Augustus' daughter, Julia. His sons, however, died prematurely; the last one was killed by Tiberius, the second emperor.

he was no less bold and quick to change plans when necessity required. Generous to his men, he relied on their skill and loyalty in the ensuing contest for mastery of the state. Not least, he wrote his own history so well that his reputation with posterity has been largely of his own design.

Caesar's conquest of Gaul took ten years (58–49 B.C.). Success made him seem more menacing than ever to the conservatives, who now sought to use Pompey as their stalking horse. The bonds that joined the first triumvirate had dissolved. Earlier, as part of the settlement, Pompey had married Caesar's daughter Julia. But she died in 54 B.C., ending what seems to have been, in spite of the appearance of expediency, a loving relationship. One year later, Crassus, the third partner, was killed and his army annihilated by Parthians at the battle of Carrhae near the Euphrates. Pompey and Caesar now squared off.

The Senate tried to persuade Caesar to give up his command in Gaul, claiming that his term had expired. Caesar refused. In Rome, two tribunes loyal to Caesar, Mark Antony and Dolabella, tried to argue his case, but at the instigation of the consuls, both optimates, they were driven out. Caesar, who was not about to put himself unarmed at the mercy of his senatorial enemies, had now found the pretext for

Left, a barbarian submitting to Romans. Such was the ideal in political art, but the new monarchy of Augustus inherited, in fact, an empire that had not successfully subdued vast numbers of Germanic tribes from the Rhine, on the borders of the Gallic province, to the Ukraine. Efforts to extend the frontier from the Rhine to the Elbe failed when, in A.D. 9, a Roman army was annihilated by the German chieftain Arminius. More than a mere setback, it meant the Germans would remain un-Romanized.

Above, the stage and backdrop of a Roman theater in Orange, France. Everywhere that Roman rule extended, provincial culture emulated that of the capital. Local grandees eagerly sought the prestige that building for the public had always conferred at Rome. Left and below, Roman tickets for entrance to the theater.

invading Italy: The sacred personages of the tribunes had been violated. On January 11, 49 B.C., he marched to the Rubicon, a small river that divided Roman Italy from Gaul. As he crossed the stream, he uttered in Greek: "The die is cast."

The civil war that followed lasted almost five years. Pompey vacillated, drawn this way and that by contending factions within his own camp. From the outset, when he inadvisedly abandoned Italy to base himself in Greece, he clearly demonstrated his limitations. After repeated offers to negotiate, Caesar finally brought him to battle at Pharsalus in Thessaly in 48 B.C. and defeated him. Pompey fled, eventually arriving in Egypt, where he was murdered by those wanting to curry favor with Caesar. That was not Caesar's style with a former ally and respected foe: He later had the assassins executed. Neither a Marius nor a Sulla, Caesar intended to reconcile rather than extirpate the opposition. But the intransigent aristocrats were to keep him at war for three more years.

By 45 B.C., Caesar was sole master of the Roman world. Even so, his soldiers felt familiar enough with him to sing as they marched in triumph through the streets of Rome: "Home we bring our bald whoremonger/ Romans, lock your wives away/ All the bags of gold you lent him/ Went his Gallic tarts to pay." Caesar's love of women had not gone unnoticed. Indeed it nearly cost him everything in 48–47 B.C., when his affair with Cleopatra kept him in Alexandria, where he was trapped and nearly killed by her brother's troops.

In 47 B.C., Caesar had been elected dictator. Two years later, he was proclaimed dictator for life and granted absolute military power in all provinces of the empire. Though the annual elections continued, only Caesar's hand-picked candidates could run. Meanwhile, Caesar instigated ambitious projects for settling veterans on land and schemes to untangle the city's traffic. He also readied himself for a campaign against the Parthians to avenge the debacle of Crassus.

It will never be known for certain whether Caesar

Romanization meant roads, theaters, and monumental arches— but also aqueducts, water closets, and baths. More than a means to cleanliness, the Roman bath was a health club and social center, growing to comprise libraries, halls for recitation, grounds for running and wrestling. Here was everything for the "sound mind in a sound body" that Juvenal praised under the early empire. Open to all at a modest fee, public baths were often lavishly appointed and were sometimes immense. The baths of Caracalla, for example, covered twenty-seven acres. Left, a cold-water basin at the end of the caldarium, or hot room, from the modest baths by the road to Stabia in Pompeii.

Leisure pursuits

A large proportion of Rome's one million or so inhabitants had plenty of free time on their hands, either because they were unemployed or because they were wealthy enough to own slaves. But even the workers and businessmen of ancient Rome finished work by noon or early afternoon. Then they might sojourn to the baths, where they would play *trigon,* a catch-ball game for three; or a form of handball, like that still played in Ireland and the Basque country; or *harpastum,* a kind of rugby. Women often played a game of *trochus,* which involved rolling a metal hoop with a tiny key. For the more sedentary, games of "petty-thieves" were always on in the public gardens, played on boards with counters of different values. Also popular was a form of backgammon. More perilous, and ubiquitous, were dice games.

Top, a tavern scene from a Pompeian fresco. Roman bars were often fronts for illegal gambling and brothels. Since "licensed" brothels were forced to remain closed until the ninth hour—about 1:00 P.M. in winter and 2:00 P.M. in summer—taverns, which remained open at all hours, frequently employed prostitutes as barmaids, with gambling rooms in the rear of the bar. Immediately above, a mosaic showing a cockfight—a bloody and popular pastime. Above left, dice, both six-sided tesserae *and four-sided* tali. *The best throw was "Venus," the worst, "dog." Loaded dice were not infrequent. Left, boys playing ball.*

planned to become king. Three times he spurned a proffered crown. But a group of Senators, who sought a return to the free oligarchy of Republican Rome, pieced together enough evidence to convince themselves that he did. The assassination of Caesar—instigated by Brutus, Cassius, Cinna, among others—brought down the man whom many considered the greatest of the Romans and provoked another bloody civil war (44–42 B.C.).

The defeat of Caesar's assassins left three men in power, a second triumvirate: Octavian, who had been adopted by his granduncle Julius; Mark Antony, Caesar's follower and lieutenant; and Aemilius Lepidus, one of Caesar's generals, who proved of little consequence in what became a two-way struggle between Octavian and Antony.

The contrast between Octavian and Mark Antony could hardly have been greater. Octavian was cold, efficient, able to suppress all desires in pursuit of power; Antony was sensual, erratic, eager for glory but easily distracted—a man who, though first and foremost a soldier, eventually achieved fame through one of history's great affairs of the heart.

The Egyptian temptress Cleopatra proved to be Antony's undoing. Antony preferred Cleopatra to his wife, Octavian's sister, and formally married her in 32 B.C. Octavian promptly accused Antony of planning to make Cleopatra queen of Rome. When the Senate declared war on the Egyptian queen, Antony responded by invading Greece. He and Cleopatra were defeated at the battle of Actium in 31 B.C.; vanquished, they committed suicide. With Antony's death, all possibility of effective opposition ceased. The Roman republic was spent.

When Octavian returned in triumph, he set about reorganizing Rome's political structure into a military autocracy, a transformation he took great pains to disguise. Indeed, he initially proposed that he resign the powers he already had. The Senate instead voted to increase his powers. He was accordingly granted control over the provinces of Gaul, Nearer Spain, Syria, and Egypt for another ten years—somewhat on the model of Caesar's Gallic command. The Senate also handed him the epithet Augustus, ("awesome," "sacred"), a title never before bestowed on a human being. Later, he was granted the powers and immunities of a tribune for life.

Though Augustus, like Caesar, continued the annual elections for the magistracies, he hand picked many of the candidates. He also gradually assumed control of the various branches of civic administration that the magistrates had overseen until, like the consuls, they were reduced to holding merely formal titles. The consulship, on the other hand, remained important as a first step to governing in the provinces, a few of which were still farmed out to members of the Senate. But Augustus kept the volatile frontier provinces of Gaul and Syria under his special jurisdiction, for that was where the majority of Rome's legions—reduced from sixty to twenty-eight after the Civil War—were based. Egypt, which was crucial for the supply of grain that placated the urban plebs, was kept under direct control.

Augustus' interests extended beyond power. Not gifted to be his own historian like Caesar, yet as mindful of posterity, he inaugurated a cultural renaissance. He sponsored the building of a theater in memory of his favorite nephew, Marcellus, and built magnificent new temples to Mars and Apollo. He also claimed to have restored eighty-two other temples that had fallen into disrepair. His general Agrippa was responsible for building the first Pantheon and for enlarging the water supply. His friend, the Etrus-

*Augustus' preferred successors died in rapid
succession—an unparalleled run of bad
luck—leaving only Tiberius Claudius Nero
(left), the eldest son of Augustus' steely wife.
Tiberius reached the throne with solid military achievements to his credit and proved a
capable ruler. He was never loved, however,
in part because he retired morosely to his
splendid villa (above) on the island of Capri,
leaving the administration of the empire to
Sejanus, head of the Praetorian Guard. Gossip about his sexual perversions was rife in
Rome. Much of it has been recorded by Suetonius, who relates that Tiberius had boys
and girls trained to perform sexual acts for
him in threes. One woman whom he forced to
his bed called him a "filthy-mouthed, hairy,
stinking old beast." Right, the emperor Claudius, Tiberius' nephew, and his second wife,
Agrippina.*

Left, a fresco from Herculaneum depicting a priestly ritual from the cult of the Egyptian goddess Isis. Roman women—and men—thronged to her worship until the end of the empire. She was known as "The Star of the Sea," "Lady of All," and "Isis of the Myriad Names." One of her hymns proclaims: "You gave women equal power with men." Another declares: "I am she whom women call goddess. I ordained that women shall be loved by men. I brought wife and husband together, and invented the marriage contract." The Senate early on attempted to stop the cult from spreading, and Christianity later found it a tenacious rival.

Gods from afar

The earliest Romans were farmers and fighters who worshiped local, practical gods, with names like "Wheat Rust," "Inner House," 'Begetter,' and "Sex." The Romans also adopted the more anthropomorphic deities of the Greeks: Mars took on the character of Ares, Venus of Aphrodite, Jupiter of Zeus. But Olympian religion was aristocratic and offered scant solace to the nameless poor. The lower classes rallied to Liber, the token of Liberty, and then to his Greek counterpart, Bacchus, whose orgiastic cult was viewed with displeasure by an aristocratic Republican Senate. The urban proletariat and new professional military class, on the other hand, found meaning in gods from the East. One of these, the Persian Mithras, was closely associated with Helios, the sun god. The emperor Aurelian built a splendid temple for the sun god, whose festival fell on December 25. In the end it was another Eastern cult, Christianity, that gained the imperial nod.

Right, an altar dedicated to the worship of Isis. Because serpents were sacred to the deity Isis, Cleopatra—who saw herself as the goddess incarnate—employed asps for her suicide. Below, a bas-relief showing a procession in honor of Isis.

Left, a statue of Serapis enthroned. A Hellenized version of the Egyptian god Osiris, the mate of Isis, Serapis was worshiped in many of the goddess' temples. Above, Mithras slaying a bull. This act of the Persian god of light was symbolic: Taurine blood indicated life, and the slaying of the bull signified the promise of life after death. The rites of the devotees were secret and conducted in underground rooms and caves. Below left, a Pompeian fresco depicting Helios the sun god. Below, the goddess Cybele, whose cult required self-castration.

Left, a coin of the emperor Galba, Nero's successor. After Nero, dynastic legitimacy vanished as a basis for power. The northern legions hailed Vitellius (below left) as emperor, but the eastern legions replaced him with their own choice, Vespasian.

can grandee Maecenas, became a byword for literary patronage. Virgil and Livy celebrated in verse and prose the glory of the empire, its heroes and its history. Horace, Propertius, and Ovid entertained the privileged with uplifting lyrics, passionately learned elegies, and witty tales of weighty loves.

Less successfully, Augustus encouraged a religious revival, refurbishing various cults and priesthoods as well as shrines. He attempted a moral crusade among the nobility, whose birthrate was declining, to encourage large families and limit sumptuous display. The women of his house continued to spin and weave according to the old aristocratic custom.

The closing years of his long reign were darkened by the scandal of his daughter Julia's alleged promiscuity, the difficulty of determining the succession, and the problems of Rome's borders. Attempts to extend the Roman frontier across the Rhine to the Elbe and consolidate Roman power in Germany came to a disastrous halt in A.D. 9, when three Roman legions under Quintilius Varus were ambushed by Germanic tribes in the gloom of the Teutoburg Forest. Years later, when the Romans visited the scene of the massacre, they found bones tangled among the dense foliage and skulls nailed to tree trunks. The German tribes remained un-Romanized —a constant source of antagonism—and eventually

Nero (above) was the last heir of Augustus. He came to power when his mother, Agrippina the Younger, poisoned her husband, the emperor Claudius, in A.D. 54. Left, the Praetorian Guard, which Augustus made his elite bodyguard in 27 B.C. The power of the Praetorians increased under Tiberius, and soon they were choosing emperors.

took part in the great barbarian invasions of the fourth century A.D. Augustus never forgot that catastrophe in Germany. For the last five years of his life, he is said to have repeated time and again, "Varus, Varus, give me back my legions."

The problem of the succession proved equally intractable. His original heirs, the sons of his daughter Julia, both died young. Augustus, who never had a son, eventually adopted his stepson Tiberius, the son of Augustus' second wife, Livia, by her former husband, Claudius Nero. Tiberius was a gloomy, dour character, and relations between him and Augustus were strained. But in A.D. 13, Augustus invested him with military authority equal to his own. When Augustus died in A.D. 14, Tiberius became emperor, the first of the Julio-Claudian dynasty.

Though Augustus found the question of succession vexing, the history of the next four hundred years shows that the well-being of the empire never really depended on the character and abilities of the emperor, whose deficiencies Rome long managed to survive. Tiberius, in spite of a promising background as a general and administrator, spent nearly half his reign as a recluse on the island of Capri. An imperial bodyguard, the Praetorians, based at Rome, had been formed by Augustus. In the absence of Tiberius, it was their captain, Sejanus, who ran affairs—for his own benefit and that of his friends, as it turned out—until he was finally checked. Meanwhile, the Parthians, those dexterous mounted archers who had annihilated Crassus' forces in 54 B.C., renewed their threats to the eastern borders. Trouble also arose on the Rhine, but still the emperor did not stir from Capri.

When Tiberius died in A.D. 37, his successor demonstrated the worst defect of dynastic succession: failure to guarantee that a man of ability would ascend the throne. Tiberius' grandnephew Caligula was a psychopath, warped no doubt by the atmosphere of intrigue and by aristocratic inbreeding. An incestuous, demented megalomaniac who spent his nights wandering the palace corridors imploring day to dawn, he ruled ineffectively for four years. According to Suetonius, Rome's gossipy historian, his only "military" exploit was to march his legions to the Atlantic coast of Gaul, where he ordered them to line up along the beach. "Gather seashells," came the instruction. The soldiers, with helmets full of shells, were marched back to Rome. Caligula then declared a great victory over Neptune, the god of the sea. His sexual whimsies so angered those around him that he was murdered by guards in A.D. 41.

Caligula was succeeded by his bald, stuttering, and middle-aged uncle Claudius. Against all expectation, he proved perhaps the most competent of Augustus' dynastic successors. Not only did he add the new province of Britain to the empire, but he admitted Gauls to the Senate, something that only Caesar before him had tried. This was a momentous step toward political integration. Behind the scenes, however, Claudius had troubles—mainly with his young

Right, Titus Flavius Vespasian. By the sole authority of his troops, Vespasian founded a new dynasty—the Flavian. Born in the hills north of Rome, he proved an able and frugal ruler. During his reign, supreme power passed from old Roman nobles to the Italian bourgeoisie. In the tradition of monumental public works, he began an amphitheater (below), dedicated in A.D. 80. Later known as the Colosseum, it became Rome's most famous structure, a symbol of the city itself.

Facing page, two contrasting views of Palestine: the arid Qumran region, near the Dead Sea (top), and the fertile region of Galilee (bottom). In A.D. 66, an outbreak of Jewish nationalism led to the massacre of the Roman garrison in Jerusalem. Vespasian and his son Titus took charge of the war against the rebels. The Jews fought tenaciously and were not finally broken until A.D. 70, when Jerusalem was captured and destroyed by Titus; the Diaspora of the Jews had begun. The Jews were generally tolerated by the Romans and suffered little persecution in the empire until Christianity came into power.

wife, Messalina. Thirty-four years his junior, she created her own state within a state, a sort of pornocracy, in which her lovers were promoted and her enemies executed. Gossip—this time from the satirist Juvenal and the letter writer Pliny—tells how she spent her evenings in a brothel, indulging her wildest sexual fantasies. Her uninhibited pastimes were eventually discovered by Claudius, who had her stabbed to death. His next wife, Agrippina, was an even more unfortunate choice: She plotted to bring Nero—her son by a previous marriage—to the throne. Her hope was realized in A.D. 54, when Claudius died—poisoned, it is said, by Agrippina.

With Nero, the period of relative sanity under Claudius gave way to a black comedy of intrigue, assassination, incest, and sexual perversion. Nero's artistic pretentions added a note of farce. He fancied himself a poet but was so insecure about his gift that he locked the gates of the auditorium during his recitals. His reign was marked by an uprising in Britain and by new Parthian invasions in the East. It ended

Gladiators

The brutality of the ancient world is perhaps seen at its worst in the gladiatorial games. Originally part of the great public funerals that enhanced the prestige of the rich, they were first produced at state expense in 104 B.C. Successful politicians and generals would reward the Roman plebs with lavish spectacles in which hundreds of gladiators and thousands of animals might die. At the beginning of the second century A.D., a spectacle was held in which 4,941 pairs of gladiators fought. When Titus opened the Colosseum in A.D. 80, the gladiatorial combats resulted in the deaths—in one day—of five thousand beasts. This insatiable need for bloodshed led to the disappearance of many wild animals from North Africa and parts of the Near East.

The main training schools for gladiators were in Capua, south of Rome. It was here that Spartacus began the great slave rebellion in 73 B.C., with a small force of seventy escaped gladiators. The combatants were characterized according to their arms, and emperors liked to pit different types against each other. Sometimes freak fights were staged: In A.D. 90, the emperor Domitian had a dwarf gladiator fight with a woman. With the triumph of Christianity, the bloody spectacle was abolished.

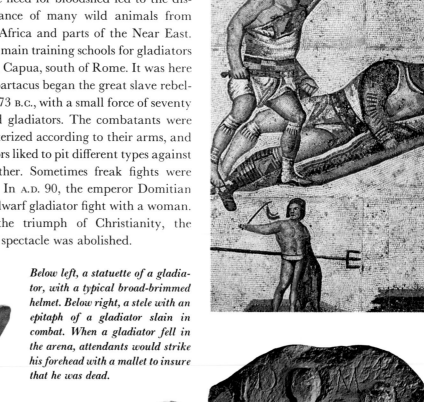

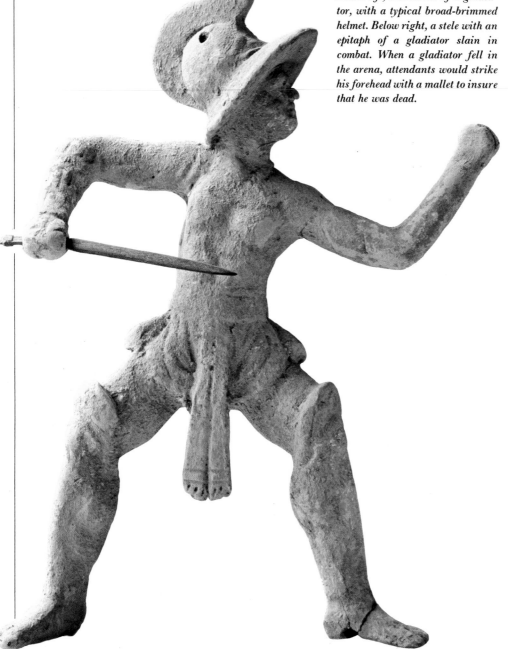

Below left, a statuette of a gladiator, with a typical broad-brimmed helmet. Below right, a stele with an epitaph of a gladiator slain in combat. When a gladiator fell in the arena, attendants would strike his forehead with a mallet to insure that he was dead.

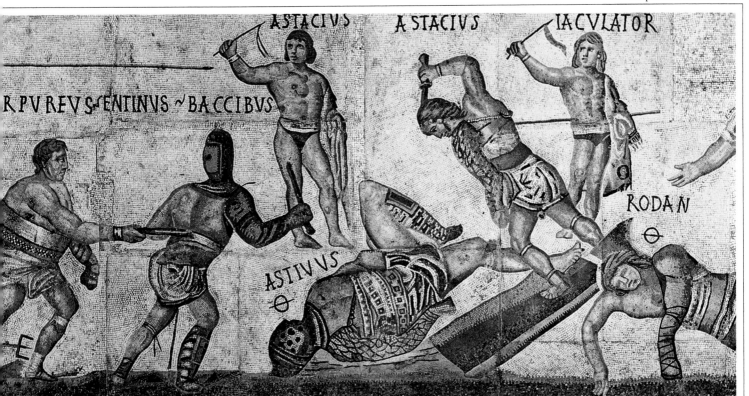

Above, gladiators fighting. The Roman taste for matches between different types of armament shows clearly. Right, a venatio, or battle between man and beast. The Romans also used beasts to dispose of condemned criminals, who were thrown into the arena with hungry lions, a spectacle devised by Augustus. The scene of many such blood baths was the Colosseum (below), which could hold ninety thousand spectators. Here thousands of Christians met martyrdom—a memory honored by the cross in the foreground.

Immediately above, a gladiator's helmet decorated with scenes from the story of Troy. This was part of the full armor worn by the so-called Samnite, who carried a large shield and a sword. Other conventional types were the Thracian, who bore a round buckler and a dagger; the "net man," who carried a trident; and the "myrmillon," who had a helmet crest in the shape of a fish and was pitted against the net man. To vary the spectacle, mounted gladiators or charioteers were sometimes pitted against each other in the arena.

Above, spoils from the temple in Jerusalem being carried off by victorious Roman troops. This relief on the arch between the Colosseum and Forum commemorates the triumph of Titus over the Jews in A.D. 70. Vespasian's son proved popular during his brief reign. Suetonius later called him "the pleasure of the human race."

when, in A.D. 68, the legions in Spain and elsewhere proclaimed their own emperors. Nero, at this news, killed himself. Dying, he exclaimed, "O what an artist dies in me!"

The dynasty of patrician nobles had thus whimpered to an end. A year of anarchy followed, during which four emperors attained the throne. None of the first three—Galba, Otho, and Vitellius, all of whom commanded only factional support—lasted more than

a few months. Power came to rest on the shoulders of Vespasian, the first member of the Italian middle class to become emperor. Neither Senator nor noble, he was a soldier chosen by soldiers. Vespasian had served in Britain and, with his son Titus, had helped crush a Jewish rebellion in Palestine that broke out in A.D. 66.

Vespasian's reign, which began in A.D. 69, was that of a practical, no-nonsense bourgeois. He replenished the treasury, emptied by Nero, by inventing new taxes, including one on the use of urine from the city toilets for industrial purposes. He further advanced the integration of the empire by enfranchising provincials on a large scale.

Vespasian ruled for ten years—a period of comparative stability. Two of his sons eventually succeeded him: Titus and then Domitian (A.D. 81–96). The latter spent a large part of his reign on the Danube

Above, stele of the Good Shepherd. Under Domitian, Titus' successor, Christians were forced to pay homage to the emperor or die. When Domitian discovered Christians within his own family circle, he dealt with them severely, executing Titus Flavius Clemens and banishing Flavia Domitilla. Below, remains of ornamental fountains in Domitian's great new palace. Following pages, Pompeii, buried by the eruption of Vesuvius in A.D. 79.

frontier quelling rebellious tribes. He gathered about him at Rome a motley collection of advisers who formed a council of state. Having bypassed the Senate in these affairs, he was strongly resented as a vulgar upstart. In fact, the old nobility was becoming increasingly impotent. Nevertheless, it enjoyed a brief resurgence when, upon Domitian's death, the Senate's choice, Nerva, became emperor. Perhaps Nerva's reign (A.D. 96–98) is best remembered for the emperor's choice of a successor: Trajan, whose rule brought the Roman Empire to its apex.

The reign of Trajan began the period of imperial grandeur that lasted until the death of Marcus Aurelius nearly a century later. Gibbon, Rome's most famous modern historian, wrote of this time: "In the second century of the Christian era, the Empire of Rome comprehended the fairest part of the earth, and the most civilized portion of mankind. The fron-

Pompeii

In the reign of the good Titus, vines and olives graced the slopes of Mount Vesuvius, much as they do today. Then about noontime on August 24, A.D. 79, Vesuvius struck. When the volcanic eruption was over, two cities had completely disappeared: Pompeii, the local seaport and commercial center, and Herculaneum, a more fashionable resort, both set on the Bay of Naples. At the juncture of south and north in Italy, Pompeii had Italic origins with some Greek and Samnite influences. Herculaneum, as its name suggests, was more Greek, though, like Pompeii, it had been harshly Romanized.

The hot mud that engulfed Herculaneum solidified, making future excavation difficult. The lighter layers of ash and cinder that sifted over Pompeii, however, left the city easier to uncover. Pompeii thus became the byword for a museum-city—all the banalities of everyday life were abruptly immortalized in volcanic ash. Much of what we know of ordinary Romans derives from Pompeii: houses, urban organization, arts and trades, brothels, gardens, even the shape of a loaf of bread.

At the time of its premature burial, Pompeii had a population of about twenty thousand. Many Pompeians appear to have been caught in hot ash, which later hardened. The organic matter decayed and left cavities. The figures that appear when the cavities are filled with plaster (far left) vividly recall the struggle and fear of Pompeii's doomed inhabitants. Near left, one of the main streets, with shops opening directly onto the narrow sidewalks. Steppingstones sheltered pedestrians from the grime of the street but allowed wagons to pass. Below left and far left, houses in Herculaneum.

Top right, a peristyle—an inner court lined with columns in the Greek fashion. Top left, a view into the garden of a house. The atrium (immediately above), the central hall of the Italic house, was lined with bedrooms and lighted by the narrow impluvium. Right, frescoes giving the illusion of spacious architecture.

Right, a statue of the emperor Trajan. Born in Spain in A.D. 53 and Spanish on his mother's side, Trajan was the first Roman emperor of provincial birth. During the reign of this warrior-emperor, the empire reached its greatest extent, coming to include the provinces of Dacia, Armenia, Assyria, Mesopotamia, and Arabia Petraea. From booty acquired in his Dacian wars, the emperor carried out extensive public works projects, such as the forum of Trajan (below). Facing page, a detail of a column describing his campaigns.

tiers of that extensive monarchy were guarded by ancient renown and disciplined valour. The gentle but powerful influence of laws and manners had gradually cemented the union of the provinces. Their peaceful inhabitants enjoyed and abused the advantages of wealth and luxury." Ironically, although he initiated the golden period of Roman peace, Trajan found it necessary to spend most of his reign campaigning on the frontiers. He created the new province of Dacia in an area stretching roughly from the lower Danube to the Black Sea after subduing tribes that had troubled the border for over a decade. He then moved east to confront the Parthians, advancing to the Tigris and capturing the Parthian capital of Ctesiphon in A.D. 114. Subsequently, he created two more provinces: Assyria and Mesopotamia. These marked the limits of Roman expansion eastward.

Trajan had come from the province of Spain. He appointed as his successor his cousin Hadrian, also from the same area. Hadrian's rule (A.D. 117–138) was characterized more by diplomacy than war. He abandoned some of the newly acquired eastern provinces and negotiated a settlement with the Parthian king. He also established the boundary of the province of Britain by constructing a long wall across its northern border.

Hadrian's twenty-one years as emperor were marked by a surge of building projects in the provincial capitals, whose architecture began to rival Rome's own. Hadrian himself rebuilt the Pantheon in its familiar domed form. More liberal attitudes were adopted toward slaves, confirming a trend

Roman aqueducts

Public works bespeak the values of society. Rome stands out not only for its attention to the tools of power but also for its interest in the amenities of civilian life. Fresh water—whether lugged home to tenements by the plebs, piped in to restful peristyles by the rich, siphoned off without payment by the unscrupulous, or enjoyed in the public baths by all—was of prime concern to Romans.

As early as the sixth century B.C., Etruscan engineers drained the Forum and showed the Romans how to channel local water. By the end of the fourth century B.C., the population outgrew the capacity of wells, cisterns, and local springs. Whatever other concerns they may have had, Rome's leaders did not neglect the issue of water supply. Appius Claudius, who built the road of dominion to the south (the Appian Way), also built the first aqueduct. Augustus, who "found Rome adobe and left it marble," nearly doubled the water supply. By the time of Trajan, eight aqueducts brought Rome an estimated 222,237,060 gallons of water daily. Throughout the empire, aqueducts attested to the skill of their engineers and the Roman values of the towns.

Top right, the aqueduct of Tarragona, Spain. During imperial times, many of the finest aqueducts were constructed in the provinces. Their characteristic striding arches were necessary to give a uniform inclination to the conduit that ran along the top. Center right, a detail of an aqueduct in North Africa, clearly showing the water channel. Below, an aqueduct built by Hadrian to supply Rome's colony at Carthage.

Above right, an arcade of the Pont du Gard, in southern France. Built in the first century A.D., this is one of the finest examples of Roman engineering. Its large central arches have a span of 82 feet, and the total height of the structure is 162 feet. The water was carried in a conduit above the third tier of arches. Below, a detail of the conduit of the Pont du Gard, showing the accumulation of calcium deposits.

Above, terra-cotta piping from Pompeii. Terracotta or lead pipes brought water from the aqueducts to public fountains, private houses, and baths. The vast majority of the population, however, had no direct water supply at home and was forced to rely on water carriers. The cost of building and maintaining aqueducts was enormous, yet no attempt was made to relate user fees to capital needs or even running expenses. For this reason, water—like bread and circuses—became yet another imperial obligation to the people.

A provincial from Spain, Hadrian (left) reduced still further the domination of Italy. Adopted by Trajan on his deathbed but already proven in public service, he spent half his reign (A.D. 117–138) in travel, consolidating and unifying his domain. Hadrian was imbued with the culture of Greece, and the Greek East hailed him as a new Panhellenic Zeus. Among the Athenians, he earned the name of "Olympian." Hadrian's temple at Ephesus (below left) was long revered.

begun under Claudius, who had decreed that any master who left a sick slave to die would be tried for murder. Hadrian abolished the master's power over life and death; now, only a magistrate could impose the death penalty on a slave.

Antoninus Pius, hand picked by Hadrian to be his successor, reigned for over twenty uneventful years. Early in his reign, a eulogist had written: "Yours is a universal empire, distinguished herein that your subjects are all free men. The whole world keeps holiday, the age-long curse of the sword has been laid aside. . . . " In spite of the hyperbole, the poet had some reasons for his praise: The empire was not threatened, and Rome, its capital, was a magnificent metropolis. The city had now expanded well beyond the old Servian boundaries, and the head of a pacified world no longer felt the need of walls. Covering an area of about eight square miles, it had a total estimated population of as much as one and a half million. The majority was housed in tenements which numbered perhaps as many as forty-six thousand in all. Some of these tenements were skyscrapers by ancient standards, sixty-five feet high. Many were slums of unimaginable squalor that stood side by side with the palaces of the wealthy and the magnificent monuments erected by the emperors.

Left, a section of Hadrian's Wall, at Cuddy's Crag in Britain. Begun after Hadrian's inspection of Britain in A.D. 122, the wall was designed to secure the northern frontier against the Caledonian barbarians. Generally moderate and successful in provincial administration, the emperor provoked rebellion in Judea by building a shrine to Rome's great father god, Capitoline Jupiter, on the site of the Jewish temple in Jerusalem that Titus had sacked in A.D. 70. In Rome, he built rich and innovative monuments, including the Pantheon, which has become a symbol of the Eternal City. Hadrian's final achievement was the adoption of Antoninus Pius (above) and subsequently Marcus Aurelius as his successors. Hadrian's successors ended the period of "the five good emperors," which began with Nerva and Trajan.

"In wreaths thy golden hair"

What slender Youth bedew'd with liquid odours/ Courts thee on Roses in some pleasant cave;/ Pyrrha, for whom bind'st thou/ In wreaths thy golden hair, Plain in thy neatness? Milton, in the tradition of Horace the Augustan lyricist, celebrates a simple hair style. Yet Ovid, writing several years after Horace, indicates that frippery flourished even in the austere climate fostered by Livia and Augustus: "Easier," Ovid says, "to count an oak's acorns than the new hair styles in a day."

So it was that taste in hair styles followed a whimsical course. In the stern Republic, the hair was parted evenly in front and gathered at the back of the neck in a knot. By Livia's time, however, braids were coming into fashion. Subtle variations in the coiffure depended on the shape of the face, according to Ovid: An elongated face required a part in the middle of the forehead, with the hair delicately framing the cheeks; a round face needed a knot on the top of the head, with the ears uncovered.

In the spirit of the ever-increasing luxury and grandiosity of the empire, the trichotectonic and comoplectic arts outdid themselves. The twisted curls and locks that rose in tiers led the poet Statius to compare a woman's headdress to a stage set. The *ornatrix,* or adorner, was a slave much prized and abused: "One curl of the whole round of hair was astray," writes the epigrammatist Martial, "badly set by a loose pin. This crime was avenged with the telltale mirror and the maid fell stricken because of the cruel locks." The new art in life forced a new liveliness on art. To keep up with the latest fashions, sculptors invented a removable marble wig—a stone worked separately from a sculpted likeness that could be changed according to occasion and style.

Roman women would often affect wigs, which were highly admired and imported en masse: blonde hair from the Germans and red hair from the barbarians in the north. On top of these fancy hairdos women set large pins, diadems, combs of bone or tortoise, ribbons, and even little

Above, Agrippina the Younger, with a comparatively simple hair style (A.D. 50). Below left, Julia Flavia and an example of the tiered style (A.D. 70). Below, Faustina the Elder (A.D. 160s), with a restrained style known in all periods.

vials containing perfume—or poison, according to the aim of the encounter in view. In the later empire, bands bordered or entwined with pearls came into vogue, a custom that we see reflected in the early products of Byzantine art. Nor were dyes lacking, even intense red, black, and ash grey. Yellows and blues were taboo, however, except for courtesans.

Above, curls gathered under a diadem—the iconography of an empress. Depicted here is Poppaea, Nero's mistress and second wife. Left, the empress Julia Domna. This coin, struck by Julia's husband, Septimius Severus, shows an elaborately curled coiffure. Top right, the wife of Trajan, the empress Plotina. Her hair style is of the tiered variety, popular at court from the late first century A.D. onward. Center right, Agrippina the Elder. The daughter of Julia and Agrippa and granddaughter of Augustus displays a curled but simple style that soon went out of fashion. Bottom right, a lady of the late Republic and early empire showing the "classic style."

Below, the column erected in Rome to commemorate the victories of Marcus Aurelius (A.D. 161–180) over the Germanic tribes of central Europe. Marcus was given to deep philosophical contemplation, which he set down in his book of meditations. As emperor, he was called on to undertake arduous campaigns against the tribes beyond the Danube. Right, Marcus Aurelius preparing to offer sacrifice.

Antoninus Pius was the last emperor who could while away his time in Rome. Barbarian pressure on the borders could no longer be ignored. Marcus Aurelius, his successor (A.D. 161–180), spent nearly his entire reign fending off the wild tribes that were once more threatening Dacia and the Danube. A Stoic by philosophy, a humble man by nature, and a general only by necessity, he was the first emperor to witness the irruption of barbarian tribes as far into the empire as northern Italy itself, which was ravaged briefly by the Marcomanni and the Quadi tribes from central Europe. At the same time, there were losses in the East, and the legions returning from service there

Below, a head of the first African emperor, Septimius Severus (A.D. 193–211). Above, Severus' son Caracalla (A.D. 211–217). Caracalla generally proved to be despotic and cruel, purging all those whom he suspected of being friends with his brother Geta, whom he had murdered. During his reign, the citizenship of Rome was extended to all free males of the empire. Right, a detail of brickwork from the enormous baths begun by Septimius but opened and named by Caracalla. An admirer of the barbarians, Caracalla took his name from a long hooded cloak worn by the Gauls that he introduced to Rome.

brought back with them a plague that decimated the Roman population. Marcus Aurelius drove the barbarians out, but the trouble spots were so numerous that he was not able to concentrate Rome's increasingly inadequate manpower in any one place long enough to achieve decisive results. Marcus died while campaigning near Vindobona (now Vienna), and his son Commodus succeeded him.

It was with the reign of Commodus (A.D. 180–192) that Gibbon chose to begin his account of the Roman Empire's decline. The underlying causes are as complex as the civilization of Rome itself. Increased barbarian pressure had become apparent during the lifetime of Marcus Aurelius. Commodus gave up the effort to quell the Germanic tribes beyond the Danube and instead used bribes to stave them off. At the same time, economic difficulties were manifest. Inflation became so serious—perhaps in part because of the cost of the border wars—that Commodus was forced to introduce a list of maximum prices for various articles. Another crisis added to the growing economic gloom and made the emperor's measures inadequate: Plague struck Rome once again in A.D. 189, killing as many as two thousand people a day.

Commodus was assassinated in A.D. 192. A year of bloody anarchy, like that after Nero's death, brought to the throne Septimius Severus, the first African-

Above, a bust of the emperor Gordian the First (A.D. 238). One of the many emperors nominated by the troops in the chaos following the fall of the Severi, he ruled for twenty-two days, then killed himself.

Below, the Roman amphitheater in Thysdrus. It was here that Gordian the First was proclaimed emperor when he was governor of the province of Africa. The amphitheater was one of the empire's largest.

born emperor. During his reign (A.D. 193–211) and that of his son, Caracalla (A.D. 211–217), inflation increased drastically. Severus responded by devaluing the imperial coinage—the silver denarii. The cost of Caracalla's wars on the Danube and in the Near East led to further devaluation, such that by the middle of the third century, banks in Egypt refused to accept the devalued currency.

Meanwhile, the frontiers were making new military demands. During the reign of Alexander Severus (A.D. 222–235), the nomadic people known as the Goths began raiding the province of Dacia. In A.D. 238, they crossed the Danube and overran the Balkan provinces of the empire, which at this time were in the throes of another civil war of succession. Shortly afterward, the Alemanni, a confederation of Germanic tribes, threatened the whole length of the Rhine frontier. The military situation was further complicated by the emergence on Rome's eastern borders of a new Persian dynasty, which in the years A.D. 223–226 overthrew the declining Parthian Empire, weakened by its centuries of strife with Rome. Between A.D. 242 and 260, the mail-clad cavalry of the Persian king Shapur I laid waste the Roman possessions in Asia Minor, defeating the legions and even carrying off the emperor Valerian.

The empire was saved temporarily by a new series of able emperors, all from the province of Illyria in

Roman agriculture

Agriculture was the social and economic base of Roman society. Small owners—citizen farmers—made the best soldiers in the Republic and were the most frugal citizens. Even at the height of imperial expansion, agriculture accounted for ninety-five percent of the revenue of the state.

From the Punic Wars on, small farmers tended to be displaced by great estates. Purchased with the spoils of conquest and worked by slaves, these estates undermined the traditional yeoman class and obviated the need for improvement in agricultural technology. During the period of relative stability from Augustus to Commodus, this slave economy produced just enough to assure its own subsistence and to supply the needs of the cities with their parasitical upper classes. In the second, third, and fourth centuries, however, the growing costs of the border wars put increasing demands on the rural economy in taxes and manpower requirements for the army. Rome's economic base gradually broke up into the entirely self-sufficient economy of the Middle Ages, the first signs of which appeared with the manor-type estates of the third century A.D.

T·PACONIVS·T·F·COL·CALEDVS·
OCTAVIA·A·L·SALVIA·

Top right, a fourth-century mosaic of a fortified farm. The breakdown of authority in the late empire forced slave and freeman alike to submit to such arrangements for security. Center right, milking and breeding sheep. Above, a sarcophagus depicting a master overseeing laborers in the fields. Left, an olive press. Right, bringing in the vintage, from the Church of St. Constance in Rome. The symbols of Bacchus (Liber), who had been the god of freedom from earthly cares, were easily incorporated into Christian iconography.

Above, a coin of the emperor Aurelian (A.D. 270–275), who was called "the restorer of the world." He saved the empire from impending disintegration after it had suffered a series of humiliating setbacks. The emperor Valerian (right), for one, had bowed to the Persian king Shapur I. Valerian was defeated and captured by the Persians in A.D. 260. Below, the Tetrapylon of Palmyra in Syria. Palmyra, which rebelled against Rome but was recaptured by Aurelian in A.D. 273, supplied Rome with mounted archers.

In the late empire, artists departed from the traditional Greco-Roman classicism. Volume and geometric line came to prevail over realistic representation (right), the new style subserving the imperial ideology. In this realistically executed sculpture done in porphyry, Valerius and Constantius embrace.

northwest Greece. Claudius the Goth (A.D. 268–270), Aurelian (A.D. 270–275), Probus (A.D. 276–282), and Diocletian (A.D. 284–305) beat back the barbarians and patched up the borders. But the fabric of power was torn. The area between the upper Rhine and the upper Danube had to be abandoned, as did Trajan's province of Dacia, the first to fall to barbarians. Economically, this was a serious blow, since Dacia was the source of much-needed gold and silver. Aurelian, who gave up Dacia, also built a new wall around the capital, an ominous sign of insecurity.

Under Diocletian, the empire created a kind of ag-

ricultural system similar to that of medieval Europe. From the time of Marcus Aurelius, increasing numbers of barbarians—defeated or otherwise—had been settling on the land as tenant farmers. Under Diocletian, these tenants became bound to the estates on which they worked. Because money had been devalued almost beyond use, the army was often paid by distribution of goods, which were requisitioned by force from reluctant landowners and peasants. Diocletian reorganized the army and greatly increased its size. He built up a network of garrison forces settled along the far frontiers and supported by strategically

Christianity

As Rome extended its dominions, new peoples submitted not only to its power but also to its gods. By the end of the third century, the cult of the emperor had become the very basis of imperial order. A few recalcitrant Judeans, however, would have none of it. In the eyes of the emperor, Judea was a province troublesome out of all proportion to its importance. Here, Christianity, in one or another sect, had proved contagious. Already in the first century there were pockets of Christians at Ephesus in the Asian province, at Corinth and Philippi in Greece, and even at Rome—enough to provide the emperor Nero with convenient scapegoats after the great fire of A.D. 64. Pliny was similarly perturbed by the Christian settlements that grew up along the Black Sea, where he was governor under Trajan (A.D. 98–117).

A unified and confident empire did not feel unduly threatened by the early Christians. By the second half of the third century, however, with imperial order in crisis, rejection of the emperor cult seemed more dangerously subversive. Harsh and methodical persecutions took place under Decius (A.D. 249–251), Valerian (A.D. 257–258), and finally Diocletian (A.D. 303–311). But martyrs bred still more martyrs, and Christianity refused to yield.

Top, the catacombs of Saint Agnes in Rome. Though early Christians preferred to bury their dead above ground, persistent persecution forced them to construct catacombs—underground passages where they also met and held mass. Left, the catacombs of Domitilla. A distant relation of the emperor Domitian, Domitilla was exiled for being a Christian. Immediately above, the loaf and the fish, Christian symbols. The Greek word for "fish" is the acrostic of Greek words meaning "Jesus Christ God's Son Savior."

The fresco (above) from the catacomb of Via Anapo depicts the blessing of the loaves. Early Christians emphasized Christ's power and wonderworking capacity rather than, as they did in later times, his suffering. Christ's power as an exorcist—a destroyer of devils—was always strongly stressed. The late-fourth-century fresco (right) from the catacombs of Saints Peter and Marcellinus in Rome shows Christ seated between Saint Paul and Saint Peter. Saint Peter may have been martyred during the persecution of Nero. Below, a detail from a sarcophagus. The scene is an agape, or fraternal banquet, one of the earliest Christian customs.

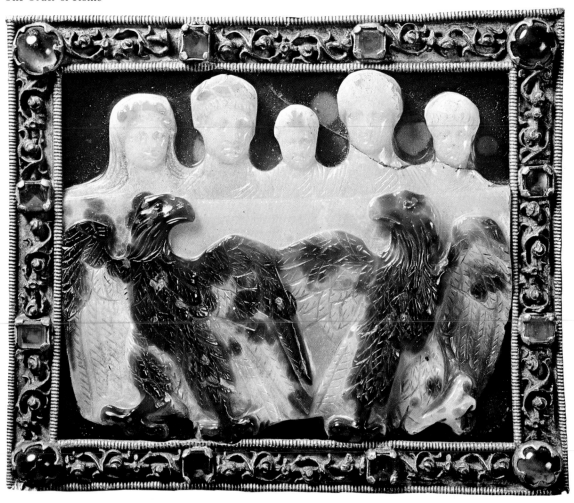

Below right, the Arch of Constantine. This and the basilica of Maxentius were among the last great monuments of imperial power to be built in Rome. Not only did Constantine's emergence as emperor presage the end of the Roman gods, but Rome itself was soon to be replaced as the seat of imperial government by Constantine's new capital, Constantinople.

Above, Constantine the Great (shown here with his family) who became sole ruler of the West by defeating Maxentius at the Milvian Bridge just outside Rome in A.D. 312. Before the battle he is said to have inscribed the chi-rho, a symbol for Christ, on the shields of his troops.

Below, the ruins of the basilica of Maxentius, Constantine's defeated rival for the Western empire. Completed by Constantine, this hall was the largest in the ancient world and was modeled on the Roman baths. Its vaults were over sixty feet in height.

placed mobile strike troops that were ready to race to any emergency. He also proposed legislation to introduce wage and price controls and set out to restructure the empire's administration. As a reorganization measure, he created two blocs, east and west, each with its own "Augustus," or emperor, and "Caesar," or subordinate emperor.

From about A.D. 286 onward, Diocletian ruled as Augustus of the East from Nicomedia, near the Black Sea. His fellow Augustus was Maximian, who ruled in the West. Their rule was blatantly autocratic—a sharp contrast to the appearance assumed by Au-

gustus two and a half centuries earlier. Diocletian's court had an elaborate ritualistic character akin to that of an Eastern king, foreshadowing the style of the Byzantine emperors. In A.D. 305, Diocletian and Maximian abdicated, and Diocletian retired to his estate on the Dalmatian coast. To those who importuned him to take up power again, he wrote: "If you could see my cabbages, you would not wish me to abandon this happy life." It is believed that he died in A.D. 316, quietly in his bed.

Unfortunately, Diocletian's reforms failed to provide for a smooth succession, and his abdication was

followed by yet another round of internal conflict. The man who eventually emerged as ruler was Constantine the Great (A.D. 312–337). Though often engaged in warfare—not only with Roman rivals but with Goths, Alemanni, and Franks (German tribes from the middle and lower Rhine)—Constantine managed to institute profound changes in the empire. He abandoned the now almost valueless silver denarii in favor of the gold solidus—setting the stage for financial stability that was to last long after the Western empire had broken up. The solidus became the currency of the Byzantine Empire and the basis of trade throughout the Middle Ages. Other reforms enacted by Constantine heralded the end of the ancient world. At Rome, he abolished the senatorial nobility by merging it with the wealthy bourgeoisie. He also disbanded the Praetorian Guard and banned the bloody gladiatorial contests.

Other initiatives were even more dramatic. Like many of the later emperors, Constantine spent little time in Rome. The emperor's presence was too often needed on the vulnerable frontiers, mainly the lower Danube region and the Near East. Constantine decided to found a new capital on the site of the old Greek colony of Byzantium. It occupied a commanding position and was close to the main theaters of action. In A.D. 324, he began building his new Rome: Constantinople.

What links the age of Constantine most strongly to the following epoch is the triumph of Christianity. By the fourth century A.D., Christianity was well entrenched at all levels of Roman society. Shortly after becoming emperor, in A.D. 313, Constantine proclaimed the official toleration of Christianity throughout the empire, and some ten years later he made it the official religion. His new capital was to be

The last defender of the old Roman gods was Constantine's nephew Julian (left), called the Apostate because he renounced the Christian faith in which he was reared. He sought during his brief reign to reestablish paganism, but his attempts left little impression. Julian saved Gaul from the barbarians in A.D. 360, but he died while fighting the Persians in A.D. 363.

Theodosius (A.D. 378–395) finally abolished the pagan cults. This painted, gold-plated medallion (below) depicts his heirs, Galla Placidia, Valentinian, and Honorius. Its lavish material and other worldly expression typify the art of the age. The empire was by this time disintegrating. It had succumbed to Christianity from the east, and now barbarians (right) assailed it in the west.

a thoroughly Christian city, in which the temple would give way to the church.

Perhaps Constantine had hoped to find in Christianity a force for unity in his realm. Instead, he discovered that the Christians were embroiled in a heated and often bloody series of theological disputes over doctrinal issues. In fact, Christianity introduced into religion an element of sectarian violence that had been largely unknown to the pagan world.

After his death, Constantine's three sons ruled the empire during a quarter century of new internal strife. Unfortunately for Rome, the new dissension coincided with a fresh wave of barbarian invasions, which were quelled only by the actions of Julian, a gifted young general who became sole emperor in A.D. 361 after the death of Constantius, the last of Constantine's sons. Julian, known to history as "the Apostate" because of his futile attempt to revive paganism, saved Gaul from the Franks and Alemanni and then marched east to deal with the Persians. His death in battle in A.D. 363 was a serious blow to Rome's hopes for survival, for the empire lost not only an able and humane administrator but also a military commander of great energy and skill.

Julian's death triggered off a chain of events that would destroy the empire in the West. Sometime toward the middle of the second century A.D., the Ostrogoths, a Gothic tribe, had established a kingdom north of the Black Sea. In A.D. 370, the kingdom fell to the Huns, nomadic Mongols that had for centuries been migrating from Central Asia. So terrifying were the Huns that the Goths believed them to be the offspring of witches and devils. The westward push of the Mongolians in turn forced the Visigoths, who had settled near the lower Danube, to cross the river. The emperor of the East, Valens, admitted large numbers of the frightened Goths into the empire, but his governors in Thrace foolishly created tension between them and the provincials. This eventually led to the disastrous battle of Adrianople in A.D. 378, which saw the destruction of the Roman army and the death of the emperor himself. As at Cannae and Carrhae, a lack of mobility and a failure to cope with efficient cavalry brought a Roman defeat. This time, however, Rome had no capacity to recuperate. The Western emperor, Gratian (A.D. 367–383), was forced to cede the Balkan provinces to the Goths.

When Gratian was murdered, Theodosius became sole emperor—the last Roman ever to do so. At his death, he was succeeded by his sons Honorius, who ruled in the West, and Arcadius, who became emperor of the East. They proved utterly ineffective, and the empire was left in the capable hands of the German mercenary Stilicho, who saved Italy from a Gothic invasion in A.D. 402. Honorius spent his life in Ravenna, at the head of the Adriatic, surrounded by sycophants and impenetrable marshlands, both of which kept him from knowing of the grim reality of what was happening to the empire. Partly as a result of this environment, Honorius had Stilicho murdered six years later, and so exposed Rome to its crowning humiliation.

In A.D. 405, a vast horde of barbarians crossed the frozen waters of the Rhine, meeting no opposition. That same year the Romans evacuated Britain, and shortly afterward, Spain fell to the Vandals, a powerful Germanic people. The seeds of the future nation-states of Europe were being planted in the fragments of the Roman West.

Rome itself was blockaded by the Gothic king Alaric and his hordes in A.D. 410. The Romans were powerless to prevent the sack of the city, which took place in August of that year. The news that Rome had fallen was shattering; it seemed to presage the end of civilization. On hearing of Alaric's triumph, the Christian scholar Saint Jerome wrote: "The brightest light of the whole world was extinguished. . . . The Roman Empire was deprived of its head. . . . To speak more correctly, the whole world perished in a city." The Dark Ages had begun.

Charlemagne and the Holy Roman Empire

The Holy Roman Empire was one of history's great paradoxes. In 1756, Voltaire caustically remarked that it was "neither holy, nor Roman, nor an Empire," and historians have been arguing with him— and with each other—about the question ever since. In theory, the Holy Roman Empire was a universal secular Christian government that was inaugurated on Christmas Day in A.D. 800, when Pope Leo III crowned Charlemagne *imperator augustus,* "great and peace-making Emperor of the Romans." On paper, the empire survived until the early nineteenth century, when Napoleon systematically dismantled it. Although its boundaries were constantly shifting, the empire at one time or another comprised all or part of

Preceding page, interior of the chapel of the royal palace at Aachen, built by Charlemagne between 794 and 806. The chapel shows the influence of both Roman and Byzantine architecture. The chandelier, a later addition, was installed by Frederick Barbarossa on the occasion of Charlemagne's coronation. Right, Charlemagne's army besieges a town. Below, a tenth-century bronze equestrian statue believed to be a representation of Charlemagne.

what we now know as France, Germany, Italy, Spain, Austria, Hungary, Poland, the Netherlands, Belgium, and Czechoslovakia.

The Holy Roman Empire was often more idea than reality. At times, there was no emperor at all; at other times, the empire existed only in writing. The disunity that plagued the empire stemmed from chronic political strife: regional and tribal conflicts; inconsistent support from the papacy (weak popes upheld the empire, strong popes tried to undermine it); the retrogressive effects of feudalism; and above all, the simultaneous emergence of Protestantism and nationalism. But even though it was in shambles

much of the time, the Holy Roman Empire endured a thousand years, and it played a crucial role in shaping the culture, politics, and attitudes that would eventually give birth to modern-day Europe.

The territory we now call Europe lay in chaos in 742, the year Charlemagne was born. The Roman Empire had collapsed centuries earlier. In 476, the last emperor of the Western Roman Empire, the timid Romulus Augustulus, had been forced to abdicate by the barbarian general Odoacer, the son of one of Attila the Hun's ministers. Meanwhile, the old empire's northern tier of provinces, which had been under firm Roman control since the days of Julius

Throughout his reign, Charlemagne led his armies in an almost endless series of military adventures. One of his most significant campaigns was against the Lombards. Above, a seal, probably of a Lombard prince. Charlemagne's victory in 774 over Adelchi (left), the son of the Lombard king Desiderius, earned him the decisive support of Pope Adrian I, who met with him afterward in Rome (below).

Caesar, had gradually cut all ties with the Eternal City and reverted to an independent status.

In Rome itself, a new institution—the papacy—slowly began to accrue power. Initially its power owed more to prayer than to the sword, for the popes' only hope of subduing the fierce tribes of the northern provinces rested in converting them to Christianity. The Church did this in miraculous numbers. But even so, many of the converted tribes refused to recognize any universal temporal authority, and they continued to engage each other in an almost endless round of petty wars. Under these conditions, Roman roads, bridges, and aqueducts—to say nothing of

Rome's celebrated social institutions—fell into ruins. Roman law, Roman governmental administration, Roman engineering, Roman arts and letters—all the hallmarks of the great empire's civilization—eroded away.

The barbarous tribes who swept down from the north were a colorful lot. One of the earliest descriptions of them comes from Tacitus, who wrote of the German warriors in the first century: "All have fierce blue eyes, red hair, huge frames." In some tribes, a young man wasn't permitted to grow a beard—the symbol of his manhood—until he had slain a foe. These tribes ultimately evolved into the peoples

Charlemagne was crowned emperor by Pope Leo III (above) in the Basilica of St. Peter in Rome on Christmas Day in the year 800. The ceremony, said to have come as a surprise to Charlemagne, officially revived the ancient empire of the Caesars in the West. Among some tribes such as the Saxons, however, the emperor's formal authority counted for little, and Charlemagne continually had to subdue them by force. Left, Charlemagne's army on the move.

Europe. As the centuries passed, one tribe came to dominate the European landscape: the Franks, who were known for their boldness and independence (the word "Frank" meant "freeman").

In the fifth century, a Frankish chieftain named Clovis united the various factions of Franks into a single kingdom, and so, in a sense, he became the first king of France. Eighteen subsequent French kings would bear his name ("Louis" is a variant of "Clovis"). Clovis' achievement was short-lived, however. The kingdom promptly fell apart in the less able hands of his descendants. Since most of Clovis' successors preferred debauchery to statesmanship, the real authority passed to the king's chief administrative assistant, the *major domus,* or mayor of the palace.

The most famous of these was Charles Martel (Charles the Hammer), who stopped the Moslem conquest of Europe at Tours in 732 in what has proven to be one of the most decisive battles in history. Although Charles Martel wasn't a king in name, he behaved like one. Before he died in 741, he bequeathed the Frankish lands to his sons. One son, Pepin the Short, ruled as the mayor of the palace, and a year after he took office, his common-law wife, Bertha, gave birth to a son. He was named Charles, after his famous grandfather, but the world would know him as Charles the Great—Charlemagne.

Few eyebrows were raised over young Charles' illegitimacy, for at this time the Franks were regarded as just a shade above pagans. After a visit to Pepin's court, Saint Boniface wrote to the pope that "the Franks are little better than heathen." However, in this period, the Church was beginning to assert its rights over the sacrament of marriage. As a result, Pepin, who needed the pope's support in consolidating his rule over the Franks, eventually had his marriage legitimized. Pepin needed the pope even more when, chafing under the title of mayor of the palace, he decided that he wanted to reign as well as rule. With the pope's help, Pepin deposed the weak Frankish king, Childeric III, and in 751 was crowned king of the Franks by Saint Boniface himself. This elaborate ceremony marked the beginning of the Carolingian line, which would take its name from Pepin's son Charles (Carolus). Pepin, a wise and cautious ruler, died in 768, and Charles, who was then twenty-six, assumed the throne.

The tasks that faced the young king were enormous. To maintain and strengthen his rule, he would lead his armies in more than fifty-three campaigns during his reign, many at the behest of Pope Adrian I, against such heathen peoples as the Moors in Spain, the Slavs, the Bavarians, the Bretons, the Bohemians,

Above, a twelfth-century stained-glass window depicting Charlemagne being received by Constantine VI at the gates of Byzantium, a meeting that never actually occurred. During the Crusades, poetic and pictorial (below) tributes ascribed fictitious heroic deeds to Charlemagne in "battle" against the Saracens, even though he died nearly three hundred years before the First Crusade.

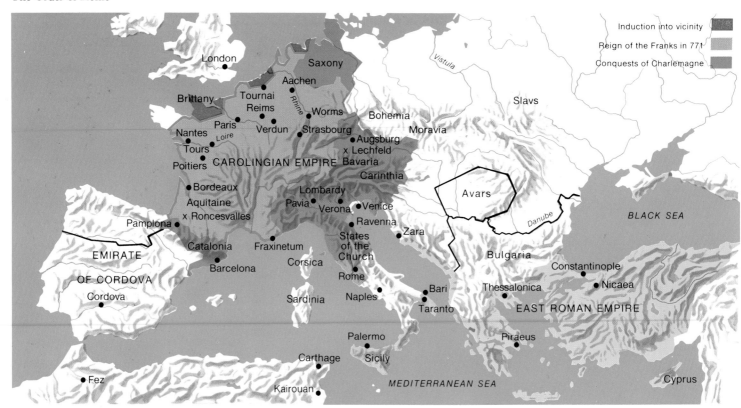

Charlemagne

Soon after being crowned emperor on Christmas Day in A.D. 800, Charlemagne began strengthening the Carolingian empire he inherited. Among those peoples he conquered were the Saxons in Bavaria and the Lombards in northern Italy. With these conquests, what was later to be known as the Holy Roman Empire began its period of expansion. This empire, based on the concept that there should be only one political leader in the world, ruling in harmony with the Church, lasted for several centuries.

Maximilian I

As king of Germany (1486–1519) and Holy Roman emperor (1493–1519), Maximilian I created an intricate system of alliances that made him an important figure in all of Europe's politics.

Charles V

Charles V, who was elected emperor in 1519, temporarily united Germany, Spain, and the Netherlands under one ruler. He eventually relinquished control over much of his realm, abdicating in 1556.

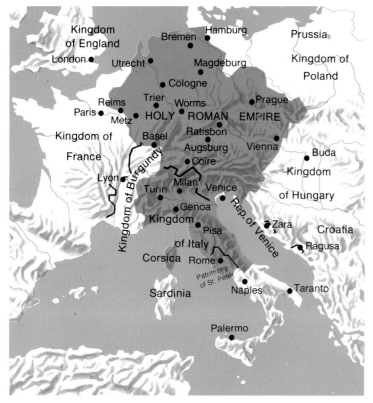

The Ottonians

When Otto I became emperor in 962, he sought to revive the weakened empire. His territory, however, was relatively small, encompassing only Germany and northern and central Italy.

The Hohen-staufens

Frederick Barbarossa was the first of the Hohenstaufen rulers. During his reign (1152–1190), the papacy-empire conflict was revived, but Frederick's main concern centered on territorial problems in Italy.

The Treaty of Westphalia

The Treaty of Westphalia (1648) marked the end of the Thirty Years' War and formalized the political disunity that had been plaguing the Holy Roman Empire. The treaty recognized the territorial independence of the German princes, according them various rights, including the right to wage war and to negotiate peace, and prevented the Holy Roman emperor from playing a role in governing their lands. This in effect signaled the end of the Holy Roman Empire.

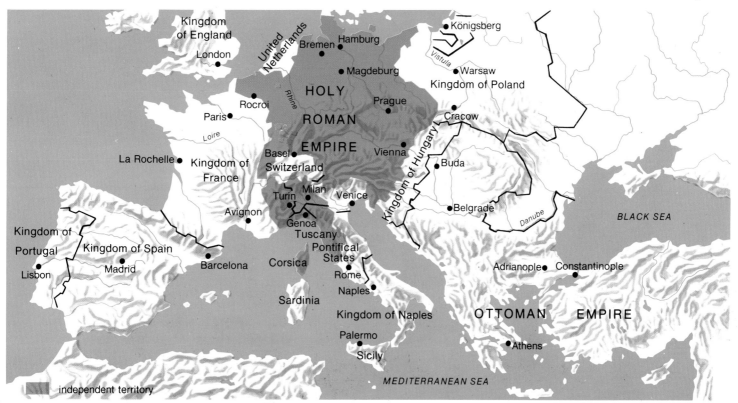

Imperial insignia

The symbols and trappings of office were of supreme importance to the empire throughout every stage of its thousand-year history. Much of the time, the authority of the emperor—as universal monarch over all of western Christendom—was more symbolic than real, and lavish ceremonies and bejeweled crowns, scepters, and swords were especially necessary to maintain at least the illusions of imperial dignity. The imperial crown (right) was made for the coronation of Otto I in 962. The octagonal shape symbolizes the Heavenly Jerusalem; the bow or arch atop it signifies world dominion. The cross stands for Christ, the emperor of heaven, whose authority on earth is invested in the man who wears the crown.

Charlemagne's sword (below) was probably buried with its owner at Aachen and removed by the emperor Otto III some two centuries later. As emperors also served as rulers of individual kingdoms, Charlemagne was entitled to wear the iron crown of Lombardy (below right), forged, according to legend, from a nail of the True Cross.

Above center, a second-century Roman gem used by Charlemagne as a seal to ratify documents. The seal emphasized the continuity between ancient Rome and the new empire. The imperial orb (above far right), now part of the imperial crown-jewel collection in Vienna, symbolized both the empire's worldly dominion (a globe) and its heavenly charter (the cross). Right, Charlemagne's white marble throne in Aachen cathedral.

and the Saxons. The pagan Saxons, who amused themselves by burning down monasteries and churches, were particularly truculent. Charles had to invade their territory in present-day Bavaria year after year before subduing them at last in 804. He was a ruthless Christian. On one occasion, he had 4,500 Saxons beheaded in a single day.

Another tribe, the Lombards, had occupied northern Italy and was threatening to capture Rome itself. Charles, who initially sought to ally himself with the Lombards, married the daughter of Desiderius, the Lombard king. He soon changed his mind about the alliance, though, and cast his wife aside in the interest of political expediency. At the urging of Pope Adrian, who pleaded with him to subdue the "perfidious, stinking Lombards," he invaded Italy and defeated a force led by his former brother-in-law, Adelchi. The victory made Charles king of the Lombards as well as king of the Franks, and it put the papacy deeply in his debt.

In 796, when Adrian died, Leo III became pope. Pope Leo was despised in Rome, where he was considered a tyrant and a rake, and soon after his accession he was attacked and beaten by a band of armed men during a religious procession. Leo's assailants left him for dead, but the pope somehow recovered and

Charlemagne's empire had no fixed capital. The emperor and his court migrated from city to city, and imperial palaces, cathedrals, and monasteries were built in scattered locations throughout the empire. Above, Trier cathedral, an eleventh- and twelfth-century Franciscan church. Top right, Lorsch gatehouse. Center right, cloister of the monastery at Essen. Bottom right, Porta Nigra, Trier. Far right, Aachen cathedral.

escaped from Rome to seek Charles' protection in the north. The king of the Franks immediately took the disgraced pope under his wing and restored him to power in Rome. When Charles went to Rome in 800, he paid homage to Leo at St. Peter's Basilica on Christmas Day. As Charles knelt before the pontiff, Leo crowned him emperor and deemed him the heir and successor to the empire of the Caesars that had ended 324 years earlier. Though Charles probably planned the coronation himself, contemporaries wrote that he was stunned and embarrassed by the

Charlemagne's chief intellectual advisers were Einhard (above left) and Alcuin of York (pictured with Charlemagne, right). Below, a page from "History of the Lombards," one of the best primary sources of the period. Below right, an initial from Alcuin's Bible. Facing page, left, Turpino and Egmeaux writing Charlemagne's biography; above right, a silver denier; below right, the death of Charlemagne.

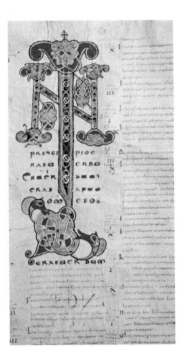

event. Charles claimed later that he would never have entered St. Peter's that day if he had known of the pope's plans.

Whatever his true feelings may have been, Charles was certainly shrewd enough to see that Leo's motives in the affair were far from selfless. By assuming the prerogative of crowning an emperor, the pope had taken for himself the highest temporal power of all—that of a king maker. Nevertheless, the deed was done. People proclaimed everywhere that the glory of the old Roman Empire had been rekindled. Europe was a political entity at last, and Charles was hailed as the new Augustus.

To his subjects, his physical stature alone was awesome. A contemporary wrote that he was "seven times the length of his foot," which meant that he was well over six feet tall at a time when the average man's height was far less than it is today. Though his culinary and sexual appetites were robust (he had five wives and many concubines in the tradition, as he thought, of David and Solomon), Charles abomi-

nated drunkenness. According to Einhard, Charles' biographer and one of the scholars in his court, he dressed simply, especially for a king. His wardrobe varied little from that of the common people. He wore a linen shirt and linen breeches under a tunic. In cold weather, he wore a snug coat of otter and marten skins. He always carried a sword.

As outstanding a general as Charles was, he proved to be an equally great administrator and delegator of authority. He saw to it that local governments in his kingdom were ruled by his own selected counts, and he appointed *missi dominici,* or royal messengers, to travel about keeping these officials under control. Charles was horrified by the prevalent illiteracy of the day and was especially scornful of the bad grammar and "unlettered tongues" of some Church officials. He urged all monasteries and cathedrals to establish schools, making no distinction between the "sons of serfs and of freemen, so that they might come and sit on the same benches to study grammar, music, and arithmetic."

Instructions such as these were issued in formal decrees, known as capitularies, or chapters of legislation, that dealt with every aspect of his kingdom—not only education but also agriculture, coinage, taxation, road and bridge maintenance, industry, and even the morals of his subjects. Not all these capitularies were obeyed, or even enforceable, but they did represent, in the words of one modern historian, "a conscientious effort to transform barbarism into civilization." Charles imposed on his many subjects one culture, one liturgy, one legal code, even a single script—Carolingian minuscule.

In his older years, Charles gathered about him the

most brilliant minds of his time. He had a splendid palace constructed for his court at Aachen, his favorite capital (there were also palaces at Ingelheim and Nijmegen), and in it he established the Palace Academy, a sort of royal literary society that met in the king's thermal baths in the palace, where weighty theological and grammatical questions were discussed. Charles brought in the famous scholar Alcuin from York, England, and from the monastery at Monte Cassino, the Lombard historian Paul the Deacon. Charles instructed Alcuin to standardize the Latin mass, and he personally saw to the preservation of many classical Latin works that would otherwise

After Charlemagne's death in 814, the empire was divided up by his son Louis the Pious among Charlemagne's grandsons, who fought each other in a civil war that lasted until 843. Facing page, above left, a coin showing Louis the Pious; below left, a carved ivory relief of a Carolingian warrior; right, Charlemagne's grandson Lothair I. This page, above, Charles the Bald, another of Charlemagne's grandsons, being presented with the Bible. Below right, a twelfth-century book cover showing Christ seated between Charlemagne and his father, Pepin, with an array of heirs beneath them.

Carolingian jewelry

During the renaissance of the Carolingian period, the art of jewelry making and metalwork flourished. The emphasis on jewelry was probably a carry-over from earlier centuries, when migratory tribes first settled Europe. To these barbarians, art meant little more than ornamentation and finery. Works of art had to be portable, and the most prized art was nonrepresentational, abstract jewelry. Gold and precious stones—especially the larger and more ostentatious gems—were highly prized. By Charlemagne's time, craftsmen had rediscovered the possibilities of pale, subdued ivory. The jewelers' artistry was most often shown in small curved boxes called reliquaries, which contained relics of saints. Chalices, crosses, crowns, buckles, rings, and brooches were other common examples. The Cross of Berengar (above), a pectoral cross with a subtle combination of gold and gems, shows how sophisticated the jewelers' art had become by the tenth century.

be lost to us today. Ironically, Charles himself had never learned to write, though he tried to learn in his old age and kept tablets under his pillow so that he could practice at odd hours. He could read Greek, and he spoke Latin exceptionally well.

Charlemagne's chief worry in his last years may have been his son and successor, Louis. Louis had proved himself a fair enough general in his father's wars in Aquitaine, but he was somewhat introspective and sincerely religious—he practiced what his father had often merely preached. Louis—known as Louis the Pious—was so religious, in fact, that Charles felt it necessary to forbid him to become a monk. Despite his reservations about his son's uncompromising piety, Charles had him crowned coemperor at Aachen in 813. Charles died the following year, after a glorious reign of forty-six years.

Now the sole emperor, Louis immediately set a different tone in the palace. He was faithful to his wife. He banished his immoral sisters from the court. He also attempted to reform the monasteries, and he became far more subservient to the pope than his father had been. As a result of his selflessness, he committed a severe political mistake: He divided his empire up among his three sons—Pepin, Lothair, and Ludwig. When his first wife died, Louis remarried and had a fourth son, known to us as Charles the Bald. Having already divided his kingdom three ways, Louis, eager to be fair, tried to redivide it to give his fourth son a share.

The three older sons objected and instigated a rebellion that lasted eight years, culminating in a battle in which Louis' own supporters deserted him. The battleground at Rotfield, near Colmar, was afterward called the Lugenfeld, or Field of Lies. Louis was taken captive, but when his three rebellious sons began to fight among themselves, two of them decided to restore him to power. Pepin, who is said to have gone insane, died in 838. Two years later, when Louis himself died, war broke out once more among the surviving sons. It was several years before an agreement was reached at Verdun. The Treaty of Verdun broke Charlemagne's great empire into three weaker fragments that roughly coincided with the present-day states of France (which went to Charles the Bald, considered the first king of France), Germany (to Ludwig), and Italy (to Lothair).

The fratricidal wars were costly. While the brothers were using their armies to fight each other, the Norse invaded the kingdom and got as far as Paris. Saracens captured Palermo and Bari, and Arabs set fire to Marseille. Amid all the havoc, the power of the kings began to erode. In succeeding generations, kings lost more respect, as the appellations their subjects gave them attest: Louis the Stammerer, Charles the Fat, Charles the Simple, Ludwig the Silent. A new ruling class arose—feudal lords and nobles, who began to act independently of the king and rule their own separate fiefdoms. In France, along with the rise of feudalism came a new, stronger French royal house—the Capetians—and France would never again be a part of the

In the century and a half after Charlemagne's death, the empire had all but ceased to exist, but it was given new life in 962, when Otto I (left), the Saxon king of the Germans, was crowned emperor by the pope. Although Otto lacked Charlemagne's cultural pretensions, he was an astute ruler, managing to unite Germany and Italy under a single monarch. Above, Otto's seal. The letters of his name are aligned in the shape of a cross.

Otto's successors tried to reunite Charlemagne's disjointed legacy, but their attempts failed. Otto II (above) died in his twenties in 983. His son, Otto III (right), shown holding a model of his church, also died young. During this time, the Cluniac order of monks was trying to bring about ecclesiastical reforms. Below, an eleventh-century manuscript showing Saint Hildefonsus, a Cluniac monk.

Unlike Charlemagne's learned court, the Ottonian court concerned itself almost exclusively with government. Culture became the province of the monasteries. The highest artistic aspirations of the society went into the construction of magnificent cathedrals. At the church and monastery of Gandersheim (left and below left), built by Otto I, lived the nun and dramatist Roswitha, who wrote long epic poems celebrating Otto I and the imperial family.

empire. Although the Carolingian line survived its founder by more than a century and a half, it is fair to say that most of its glory died at Aachen with Charlemagne.

The nobles of Germany, realizing the need for a central national power, gave the German throne to a Franconian duke, Conrad I. Conrad spent most of his seven-year reign battling a Saxon duke, Henry, whom he was nevertheless farsighted and generous enough to name as his successor. Ironically, the very Saxons Charlemagne had fought were now furnishing the king who would begin restoring the empire.

Henry's son, Otto I, who became emperor in 962, was responsible for the resurgence of the empire. Otto, known as Otto the Great, has been called the Charlemagne of Germany. Though he lacked Charlemagne's intellectual and cultural ambition, he was a strong-willed and clever ruler. By a series of shrewd political maneuvers, he succeeded in winning the loyalty of the German feudal barons and fused their separate fiefdoms into a moderately coherent state. With Germany in his grasp, he cast his eye on Italy—a ready target.

Italy's king, Berengar II, was involved in a dispute with the reigning pope, John XII. John, who had become pope at the age of eighteen, was a wastrel. He not only gambled at dice but prayed for the devil's aid while doing so. He appointed a ten-year-old boy as a bishop. He had a deacon castrated. He committed incest with his sisters. Finding himself in need of help in his struggle with the Italian king, John decided to secure an ally by crowning an emperor. Otto, happy to oblige, came to Italy with his army and was made emperor in 962. (Although various pretenders had claimed the imperial throne since the collapse of the Carolingians, none had assumed real power.) Otto now ruled all of Germany and most of Italy. Pope John, for his part, soon began to regret Otto's dominance and complained bitterly of it. Otto simply

Hildesheim in lower Saxony had its golden age under the Ottonians. To counter the growing power of the German nobles, the Ottonian emperors favored the ecclesiastical officials; the bishops of Hildesheim eventually achieved princely status. St. Michael's church (top), considered the most important Ottonian church, was begun by Bishop Bernwald of Hildesheim around A.D. 1000. Goslar (immediately above), founded in 922, was for all practical purposes the capital city of the empire until 1125. At Ottmarsheim in France, the octagonal Convent Church (left) was consecrated by Pope Leo IX in 1049.

Agriculture

Agriculture formed the economic basis of medieval society. Nine out of every ten men worked in the fields as peasants. Much of what they produced had to be turned over to the landowner—either a feudal lord or a monastery. The peasant was bound to the soil and could not leave the manor estate without the lord's permission. Those who attempted to escape could be tried and punished, the landlord himself acting as judge. If the landlord sold his fields, the peasant had to build his own dwelling—usually a crude, one-room hut—and make and repair his own tools. The light plows the Romans had used in the Mediterranean area were unsuitable in the less fertile northern lands, and a heavier iron plow was developed which cut a much deeper furrow. A stiff-collared harness was also devised, enabling a horse to pull a plow without choking, which resulted in a remarkable increase in efficiency (a horse could plow three times as much land as an ox). The most revolutionary innovation was the three-field system of crop rotation. The Roman two-field system had left half of the usable land unproductive each year. The medieval peasant discovered that wheat or rye could be sown in the autumn as well as in the spring, thus doubling the annual yield. Under the new system, one area was planted with rye or wheat in the fall and harvested the following summer; a second area planted with barley, oats, and pease was harvested in the spring; a third area was left fallow. Despite the increased yields, the work continued to be as hard and unremitting as ever. The role of the serf in the Middle Ages was purely economic—a forced consumer in times of glut, a producer at other times. His body was, by a legal fiction, capable of being divided and sold to different lords. Whatever he possessed was deemed to have been lent to him for the discharge of his tasks and had to be returned upon his death. The Church, which demanded a tithe, or tenth, of the peasants' crops, provided the only respite: "Our oxen," the peasants said, "know when Sunday comes, and will not work on that day."

Medieval manuscripts give a picture of daily life. Above, the gathering of honey. Fruit trees (right) were systematically cultivated and pruned. The arable farm land on a lord's estate (below) was divided among individual peasants into small strips that were plowed separately. Each peasant might be responsible for two or three of them scattered throughout the estate.

The medieval manor was a self-sufficient economic entity. All food was grown on the estate, and all tools and clothing were made there as well. Except in times of famine, the peasants' diet was for the most part wholesome. Meat, dairy, and poultry products were staples. Above, a peasant milking sheep. Above right, gathering eggs. Right and below right, farmers in the field planting and plowing.

Below, peasants gathering grapes for wine.

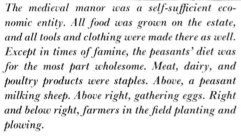

Professions

As agricultural production improved and the population of Europe increased, new villages and towns sprang up. Craftsmen moved from the overpopulated manors into these trade centers. Merchants formed associations, or guilds, that gave them monopolies on trade by setting tolls and tariffs on goods brought into the cities from outside. Artisans, craftsmen, and other tradesmen, such as tailors, barbers, stonemasons, carpenters, shoemakers, and apothecaries, formed exclusive guilds. These guilds protected their own reputation and the public by insuring that only qualified craftsmen could provide goods and services. Young men entered the guild only after a long and thorough apprenticeship—usually seven years. Eventually, the guilds acquired so much power that the actual governing of the city fell into their hands. From the guilds, a new class—the bourgeoisie—would rise up to challenge the authority of the empire.

As a result of increased trade, money came back into circulation, bringing with it the need for bankers (below).

Left, a butcher slaughtering cattle. Below, a weaver works at a loom. In Flanders and Italy, the wool guilds became so prosperous that entire factories were set up to house all the stages of textile production—washing, dyeing, spinning, weaving—under one roof. Wholesale cloth merchants provided the capital and equipment.

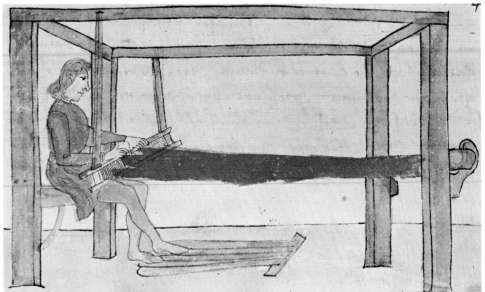

Above, craftsmen under the protection of Mercury, the Roman god of commerce: copyist, watchmaker, armorer, painter, sculptor, and organ maker. Top right, fishermen hauling in a catch. Center right, a mason laying bricks. Bottom right, artisans working with a burin, or engraving tool. Traveling merchants (below), who risked being robbed or killed on the roads, were a crucial trade link between cities.

The cathedral of Spires (preceding pages), begun in 1030 by the emperor Conrad II, is considered the finest achievement of German Romanesque architecture. The castle of Wartburg in Thuringia (left) was built by the independent German barons as a stronghold against the emperors. Here, Martin Luther later translated the Old Testament into German. Below left, Conrad II and his wife, Gisela, kiss the feet of Christ. Facing page, the imperial palace at Königlutter.

had him deposed and replaced him with a friendlier pontiff.

Otto had won this particular contest, but the people of Rome resented being under the thumb of a German, and the rivalry between emperor and pope would continue for centuries. Otto's successor, Otto II, tried to annex southern Italy to the realm but died while still in his twenties. His son, Otto III, was crowned in 983 at the age of three and began to rule at sixteen. He too died young and without leaving an heir. A Bavarian cousin, Henry II, succeeded him; Henry also died childless and was the last of the Saxon line.

Conrad II, a descendant of Henry I's old opponent Conrad, became emperor in 1024 and began a new dynasty—the Salians. Under Conrad's son, Henry III, the empire reached what may have been the zenith of its power. An intensely devout and peace-loving ruler, Henry busied himself with purifying the monasteries by supporting the new, reform-minded Cluniac order of monks. He built a splendid imperial palace at Goslar, and he ordered the completion of the magnificent cathedrals of Mainz, Worms, and Spires. Henry detested simony—the selling of church offices—and he was probably the only medieval emperor who wasn't guilty of it. Most important, he strengthened the office of the pope during his reign by filling four papal vacancies with strong, independent prelates.

Henry IV, who succeeded him at the age of six, came to regret bitterly his father's preference in popes when he found himself locked in combat with perhaps the most controversial pope in the Church's history. Gregory VII, known as Gregory the Great, became pope in 1073 and immediately asserted his temporal authority: "If the pope is supreme judge in spiritual matters," he wrote to a friend, "why not also secular matters?" Since Charlemagne's time, bishops had been selected by kings and emperors—often for a price. Gregory found this practice of lay investiture inconsistent with the Church's dignity and issued decrees against it, and against simony and clerical marriage as well.

Henry, whose own vested interest rested on selecting bishops for himself, resisted the decree, and Gregory excommunicated five bishops who served as

The Salian dynasty, begun by Conrad II in 1024, ruled the empire for more than a century. Conrad and his son, Henry III, built the monumental castle of Nuremberg (above left) to serve as an imperial residence. Immediately above, interior of the cathedral of Worms, built under Henry III, where the Concordat of Worms was signed in 1122, putting an end to the struggle between the empire and the papacy over feudal investitures. Top, Henry IV and his court. Left, the courtyard of the fortress Runkel am Lahn, built in the thirteenth century to control the nearby town of Limburg.

Henry's counselors. Henry declared Gregory deposed, referring to him by his given name of "Hildebrand, not pope but false monk." Gregory responded by branding Henry anathema, excommunicating him and, in February 1076, declaring him deposed in turn. Although Henry had armies and weapons and Gregory had only moral persuasiveness to rely on, Henry's position proved the weaker in the face of outraged public opinion. Even the Saxons under Henry revolted, and the emperor found himself helpless. He decided to seek out Gregory in person and beg for absolution.

Finding Gregory was a problem, for Gregory had fled Rome and had found refuge in the Apennine village of Canossa, at the castle of his friend the beautiful Matilda, countess of Tuscany. At Canossa, one of the most dramatic events of the Middle Ages took place—a decisive confrontation between the pope and the emperor. Henry left his army behind and arrived at Canossa with a small retinue. Gregory himself described what took place next: "He presented himself at the gate of the castle, barefoot and clad only in wretched woollen garments, beseeching us with tears to grant him absolution and forgiveness." For three days, Henry knelt on the castle steps in the snow begging to be forgiven. Finally, Gregory relented and, in his words, "received him again into the bosom of Holy Mother Church."

The pope's treatment of Henry angered the Germans, and his victory proved to be more symbolic than substantial, for Henry soon returned to Germany, regained the support of his nobles, and in 1084 arrived in Rome with an army. Gregory excommunicated Henry again, but instead of garnering support for this act, Gregory was driven out of Rome. He found refuge in Salerno, but he had lost the will to fight and the desire to live. His spirit broken, Gregory announced, "I have loved righteousness and hated iniquity, wherefore I die in exile."

Had he been able to see into the future, he might have taken comfort, for although Henry had won this particular duel of nerves, the papacy would ultimately have the upper hand, a supremacy symbolized for all time by the fateful meeting at Canossa. Ironically, the impetuous Henry IV was also to die in exile, for his own family turned against him as a result of his support of Gregory's successor, Clement III. In 1105, Henry's son forced his father to abdicate. Henry died at Liège in 1106, unrepentant and still excommunicated, but the people of Liège, in defiance of Church authority, gave him a royal Christian burial anyway.

During the reign of his son, Henry V, the conflict between pope and emperor over lay investiture was

Above, a miniature from the manuscript De-cretum Gratiani, *the Church's first systematic collection of canon laws, compiled by the monk Gratian (ca. 1140). It shows Christ conferring dual power upon the pope and the emperor. Below, an order by Andelasia, countess of Calabria and Sicily, giving instructions for the defense of a monastery against Saracen pirates. It is the oldest European document of its kind on paper.*

Henry IV at Canossa

Perhaps the supreme dramatic encounter in the medieval conflict between Church and state occurred in 1077 between Pope Gregory VII and Emperor Henry IV at the village of Canossa near Parma, Italy. Gregory had issued a proclamation banning lay investiture, but Henry refused to comply. Gregory responded by excommunicating Henry. In the ensuing struggle, Gregory was able to turn Henry's own nobles in Germany against him, and Henry was forced to seek out the pope, who was staying at Canossa in the castle of Matilda of Tuscany. For three days, the emperor, barefoot and dressed in sackcloth, knelt outside the castle in the snow begging Gregory's forgiveness. At length, Gregory forgave him, and the emperor, promising to forego lay investiture, returned to Germany to deal with his rebellious nobles. Although Henry, who later gained public sympathy, eventually went back on his promise, the events at Canossa symbolized forever the subservience of state to Church.

Right, Matilda of Tuscany accepting her biography from her biographer, Doninzone. The countess was the most powerful landowner in central Italy in the eleventh century, but at her death her lands fell into the hands of Emperor Henry V.

M ATHILDIS LUCENS. precor hoc cape cara volumen

Left, the ruins of the tenth-century castle of Matilda of Tuscany, near the village of Canossa. The memory of the political impact of the meeting there between pope and emperor lasted for centuries. Eight hundred years later, when the German chancellor Otto von Bismarck came into conflict with the Catholic Church, he vowed he would "never go to Canossa."

Above, Matilda's seal. Facing page, bottom, two scenes from the struggle between Henry IV and Pope Gregory. The one on the left shows Henry and his antipope, "Clement III" (Guibert, archbishop of Ravenna), enthroned in Rome while Pope Gregory is being driven from the gates of the city. The scene on the right shows Gregory dying in exile at Salerno in 1084.

Before he became pope, Gregory VII (above) had gained renown as a reform-minded Benedictine monk. Gregory's papacy marked a turning point in Church history, for he paved the way for a later victory on the lay-investiture question in the Concordat of Worms.

Right, Pope Gregory's adversary, Emperor Henry IV, depicted on a silver shrine containing most of Charlemagne's remains. Henry's reign was undermined by the papacy and the German nobles. The nobles at first supported Henry in his fight to retain lay investiture, but when the pope excommunicated him, one group of nobles insisted that he beg for absolution. Henry died in exile—in 1106, after his own son, Henry V, forced him to abdicate.

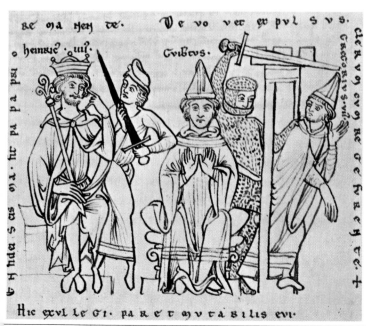

Feudalism

After the deterioration of Charlemagne's empire, most of the political power passed into the hands of the nobles. The consequence was feudalism—a primitive system that varied greatly from region to region. The nobles, or lords, held fiefs, generally consisting of landed property, which could be as large as a kingdom or as small as a manorial estate. In some areas, a fief might consist merely of the right to collect taxes and duties. A feudal lord could be as powerful as a king or duke, or he might be a knight who ruled only a village or less. Under a rigid social hierarchy, the noble who granted the fief was the suzerain, or overlord, and the noble who received it was the vassal. To receive the fief, the vassal knelt before the suzerain and swore an oath of fealty which bound him to be loyal and to perform certain services. Often these services were military, but sometimes the vassal would have to give the lord money. The feudal contract benefited both parties: The suzerain gained armed warriors and the vassal gained the use of the land and the suzerain's protection in times of civil turmoil. By a process known as subinfeudation, the vassal himself could grant portions of his fief to lesser nobles and become a suzerain of sorts in his own right.

Falconry (above) was perhaps the chief leisure-time activity among nobles in the Middle Ages. In fact, this highly complicated sport became so fashionable that in some circles a noble wouldn't dream of appearing in public without a hawk on his wrist as a mark of dignity. Even bishops and abbots became enthusiasts. They would sometimes display their birds on the altar steps during mass.

The investiture of a youth into knighthood (below left) was the culmination of long years of apprenticeship in the arts of war and chivalry. Training began at the age of seven, when a page was chosen to serve a knight. At fourteen, the page became an esquire and received a sword, although he could not wear it girded at his side until the actual investiture ceremony. Below, a medieval banquet.

The ancient fortress of Carcassonne in southern France (left) was one of the architectural marvels of Europe. When it was completed, Carcassonne was widely considered impregnable. Typically, such castles were the feudal lord's residence and the administrative and judicial center of the territory.

Below, two knights jousting in a tournament. Tournaments provided sport and spectacle for the onlookers and fame for the participants, but they also functioned as war games, offering invaluable practice in the arts of combat. The rules were very formal and strict. The participants charged each other on their mounts; the lances were, in theory, to be aimed only at the opponent's shield, not his body. Once unhorsed, the knights dueled on foot until one of them formally surrendered on bended knee.

renewed with even more vigor. Henry V refused to cease his blatant wheeling and dealing in bishoprics. He went so far as to have himself crowned emperor by brute force, imprisoning the pope and the cardinals. Eventually, like his father, he was excommunicated for supporting an antipope, though he was finally reconciled with the Church in 1122, when he and Pope Calistus II settled the issue of investiture with the Concordat of Worms. Henry, the last of the Salian line, died without an heir.

The German nobles immediately took advantage of the succession dilemma and proposed that they elect the man who would wear the crown. They were divided into two opposing political factions, the Welfs (the papal party) and the Ghibellines (the imperial supporters). After intense debate among themselves, they elected Lothair, a Saxon duke, as the next emperor. Upon Lothair's death in 1137, the German nobles elected Conrad III, of the illustrious Hohenstaufen family, to the throne. Conrad went off on the

Second Crusade with Louis VII of France to recover the Holy Land and took part in the siege of Damascus. The siege failed, and Conrad returned home in ignominy.

Conrad's nephew and successor, Frederick, became king of the Germans when he was thirty and at once staked an outspoken claim to the empire. Frederick saw Germany and Italy as a sacred entity established on earth directly by God. He referred to the empire not merely as the Roman Empire but as the *Holy* Roman Empire. Frederick was physically unimposing—short, fair skinned, and yellow haired—but he did sport a ferocious red beard that led the Italians, who lived in fear of his invading armies, to call him Barbarossa.

Following a well-established tradition, Frederick Barbarossa got hold of the imperial crown by bargaining with the pope—or in this case two popes, Eugene III and his successor, Adrian IV. In 1153, Frederick agreed to help Pope Eugene suppress a rebellion of the revolutionary commune of Rome

Above, Frederick Barbarossa and the arch-bishop of Cologne in Rome for Frederick's coronation. The day after the ceremony, the independent-minded republicans of Rome, who were not enthusiastic about being ruled by a German, rioted in protest. Bitter fighting broke out in streets, and both the emperor and the pope were driven out of the city. Frederick invaded Italy six times in the hope of subduing the rebellious city-states. Right, Maria Laach. Dedicated in 1156, this Benedictine structure is an excellent example of a medieval German monastery.

led by Arnold of Brescia, an Italian monk and reformer and a champion of the Italian city-states. When Eugene died, Pope Adrian took up the cause that opposed the arrogant city-states, and he turned to Frederick Barbarossa for help. Frederick and his armies entered Italy in 1154, and by the following year the rebellious Arnold had been executed. Now, only one obstacle stood in the way of Frederick's ambition to be crowned emperor.

Frederick met Pope Adrian at Nepi, near Rome, where the pope rode up to him on horseback. According to traditional protocol, Frederick should have led the pope's mount by the bridle and held his stir-rup while he dismounted. This ceremony, called *strator*, was a symbolic recognition of the pope's superiority over a mere temporal king. In this instance, to the shock of onlookers, the pontiff sat waiting on horseback while the king made no move whatsoever to grab the stirrup. Finally, the offended pope had to get off the horse by himself. He refused Frederick the traditional "kiss of peace," as well as the imperial crown. For the next two days, Frederick and Adrian argued endlessly over this item of protocol until Frederick at length swallowed his pride and gave in. Then the pope went off some distance, got back on the horse, and rode in again. This time, Frederick

dutifully held the bridle and stirrup of the pope's horse as the pope dismounted. Frederick was then crowned emperor and was free to do as he pleased.

The Holy Roman emperor was also, in name, the king of Lombardy, although in fact no German ruler since Henry IV had even tried to control the Lombards. Frederick Barbarossa took his title seriously, and in 1158 he sent ultimatums to the towns of northern Italy asserting his royal prerogatives, which included the right to tax the Lombards to fill his German coffers. Unfortunately for Frederick, northern Italy was commune country, and Milan, Brescia, Cremona, and other city-states had been accruing

their own power since the tenth century. Although a few towns gave in to Frederick, others, Milan among them, preferred independence.

Frederick led his army to Milan and put the city under siege. The inhabitants within the walls resisted for two years. When Frederick finally captured the city in 1162, he burned it to the ground. This so infuriated the other cities of northern Italy—Bologna, Ferrara, Padua, and Cremona—that they banded together in 1167 to form the Lombard League. The pope, caught in the middle, decided to take his chances with the rebellious cities and excommunicated Frederick. In 1176, at the battle of Legnano, the

Daily life

The rhythm of daily life in a medieval city was governed by the light of the sun. No one cared what time it was—only how much daylight was left. Church bells rang at three-hour intervals beginning at dawn, when artisans and tradesmen would rise and set about their work and servants and housewives would line up for water at the town well. Horses and donkeys congested and befouled the narrow, unpaved streets, which became virtual mud troughs after a rain. Geese, pigs, pigeons, dogs, and cats ran loose as ever-present scavengers. All was not grim, however. Shops and buildings were brightly painted, and colorful signs advertised the occupant's trade—a unicorn for a goldsmith, a horse's head for a harness maker, a white arm with red stripes for a surgeon-barber. Shops were enclosed with shutters that opened horizontally into the street: The upper shutter served as a canopy, the lower shutter served as a counter for goods and foods, tantalizing passersby with their sights and smells. Peddlers hawking milk and cheese roamed the streets singing snatches of doggerel (forerunners of today's commercial jingles) about their wares. At sunset, people returned to their houses. All cooking was done over an open fire. Broths, stews, roasts, and fish were the main courses, augmented with fruits, pastries, and spiced wine. (Tomatoes, squash, corn, noodles, rice, chocolate, coffee, and tea were unknown, and only the wealthy could afford pepper.) With the onset of night, the gates of the city were locked shut, leaving only nightwatchmen and thieves to roam the unlit streets.

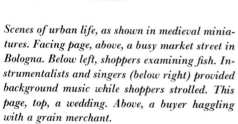

Scenes of urban life, as shown in medieval miniatures. Facing page, above, a busy market street in Bologna. Below left, shoppers examining fish. Instrumentalists and singers (below right) provided background music while shoppers strolled. This page, top, a wedding. Above, a buyer haggling with a grain merchant.

Above and below, two domestic scenes. In the daytime and evening, all activity centered on the hearth. Members of the household prepared and ate their meals and carried on tasks like sewing, spinning, and weaving. The hearth also provided needed illumination, for even on a bright day the narrow windows covered with oiled parchment admitted little light.

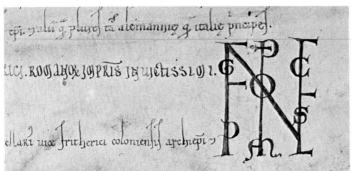

army of the Lombard League defeated Frederick's German troops. At the Treaty of Constance in 1183, Frederick agreed to the independence of the Lombard cities, while they in turn formally acknowledged Frederick as their supreme ruler, at least in theory. Under the treaty, all the Lombards were required to do was pay Frederick's expenses when he and his retinue happened to visit Italy.

Frederick had better luck at home in Germany, where he secured nearly full control over the German bishops. They were at times more loyal to him than to the pope. He defeated Henry of Saxony and destroyed the Welf power. He also established a new class of imperial civil servants to administer the German cities. Frederick staged elaborate festivals with lavish costumes and colorful pageantry that celebrated chivalry and knighthood—all of which won him the hearts of the pomp-loving Germans.

It was the love of chivalry that led Frederick to undertake, at the age of sixty-seven, the Third Crusade. The Moslem leader Saladin had captured Jerusalem two years before, in 1187, and Frederick felt it incumbent upon him in his holy office to recapture the Holy City for Christianity. Some historians think he may also have hoped to unite both the Eastern and Western empires in a new kingdom that would be as vast and powerful as the ancient Roman one. Frederick Barbarossa took off at the head of one hundred thousand men, but his army was attacked by guerrilla bands of Turks along the way. Many of his soldiers starved to death. The old emperor never reached Jerusalem; he drowned while crossing a river in Cilicia. It was hardly a glorious death for a chivalrous knight.

Frederick Barbarossa's son, Henry VI, journeyed to Rome to be crowned emperor by Pope Celestine III in St. Peter's in 1191. Like his father, Henry had glorious dreams of empire. He wanted to recover not only Italy but France and Spain besides. However, he

Frederick's son Henry VI (above left) added a new kingdom to the empire by marrying Constance, heir to the throne of Sicily. Above, the journey of Henry to Rome, where he was crowned emperor in 1191 by Pope Celestine III in St. Peter's. Henry is shown being anointed and receiving the symbols of his office—sword, scepter, ring, crown, and miter. When Henry died six years later, Constance (whose seal is seen at left) decided to raise their son, Frederick II, in Sicily.

died young, having gotten no farther than Sicily. His accomplishments there were impressive nonetheless. He managed to subdue the Normans, who had ruled Sicily and southern Italy for sixty years. To further strengthen his grip on the kingdom, he married Constance, the defeated Norman heiress to the Sicilian throne. The marriage made Henry king of Sicily as well as king of the Germans and emperor. At that moment, the empire united Poland, Bohemia, Austria, Holland, and Switzerland, as well as Germany and most of Italy (except for the Papal States, which remained in the pope's power).

The inscription in the image reads:

† IN NOCENTIVS EPS SERVVS SERVORV DL DILECTIS FILI... PRIORI ET FRIB IVXTA
SPECV BEATI BENEDICTI REGLARE VITA SERVANTIBVS ID ... INTER HOLOCAVSTA
VIRTVTV NVLLV MAGIS EST MEDVLLATV QVA ID OFFERTVR ALTISSIMO DE PINGVEDINE
CARITATIS. HOC IGIT ATTENDENTES CV OLI CAVSA DEVOTIONIS ACCESSISSEM AD LOCV SOL...
VRE IVE BEATVS BENEDICT SVE CONVERSIONIS PRIMORDIO CONSECRAVIT ET IVE... VOS IDE SECD...
IN STITVTIONE IPIVS LAVDABILITER DNO FAMVLANTES: NE PRO TE ORALIS SVBSTEN...
SPIRITVALIS OBSERVANTIE DISCIPLINA TORMERET APOSTOLICV VOBIS SVBSIDIV ...
IM PENDENDV, SPERANTES ID IDE BEATISSIM BENEDICT NRE DEVOTIONIS AF...
ET PRECIB APVD PIISSIMV PATRE ET IVSTISSIMV IVDICE COMMDABIT ...
NECESSITATIB PVIDERE: SEX LIBRAS VSVALIS MONETE VOBIS ET SVCCESSORIB VRIS DE

Pope Innocent III (above) served as guardian of the four-year-old Frederick II, who became perhaps the best-educated ruler of the Middle Ages. Left, a page from Frederick's Trac-tatus de arte venandi cum avibus, *a tract on hawking and on birds in general, considered the first work of modern ornithology. Facing page, a Sicilian mosaic of Frederick's coat of arms.*

Constance, who had been secluded in nunneries in Palermo for much of her life, was thirty when she married the twenty-year-old Henry. For twelve years, she tried to bear him an heir and failed. When, at forty-two, she finally became pregnant, legend has it that she was so proud of the fact that she had a tent erected in the marketplace of a village near Ancona and gave birth to her baby in full view of the bewildered local villagers. (Nineteen cardinals and bishops also showed up for the occasion to make certain that the baby was really hers.) Presumably, the villagers and prelates were duly impressed. They had every right to be. The infant, Frederick II, would become one of the most extraordinary and enigmatic rulers of all time.

Henry died in 1197 when his son was three, and the provincial Constance, who wanted to keep her child with her in Sicily, renounced her son's claim to the German throne— a gesture that at once threw three generations of careful empire building into chaos. The following year, Constance herself died, after instructing in her will that her son be entrusted to the guardianship of the one man least likely to have any sympathy for a future emperor—Pope Innocent III. Innocent, naturally, was delighted by the choice. He had no intention of returning the child to his father's kingdom in Germany and saw to it that Frederick remained out of the way in Palermo, where he grew up more or less on his own. Officially, he was a resident of the palace, but he was not closely supervised or cared for. Denied a systematic education, the child picked up much of his knowledge on the streets. It was an education unlike that of any other medieval ruler in Christendom.

Palermo had been held by the Moslems for two centuries before the Normans conquered it. The city was a melting pot that contained the best elements of three cultures—Jewish, Christian, and Islamic. The child learned Arabic, Latin, and Greek (he would eventually speak nine languages), and more important, he became an avid student of the city's Moslem culture. At the time, Islamic science and learning easily surpassed that of Europe. In an age when the confines of Christian dogma were absolute, Frederick received a far broader education than any royal tutor could have provided. He learned to evaluate and compare different religions and societies without prejudice.

The child may have been a pauper at times, but he was also the lawful king of Sicily, and he knew it. At the age of twelve, he abruptly dismissed the deputy regent who had been chosen by the pope to rule in his

name. The youth still lacked a power base, so three years later, when he was fifteen, he married Constance of Aragon, a much older woman whose appeal may have been her dowry—a troop of knights. With these knights, Frederick imposed his rule over Sicily. Luckily for Frederick, the current German king and emperor, Otto IV, had angered the pope and been excommunicated. Frederick was suddenly designated king of the Germans. The pope, in recommending Frederick to the German nobles, said that his ward was "as old in wisdom as he is young in years."

There was a catch, however. Frederick had to give his word to the pope that he wouldn't attempt to unite the kingdoms of Germany and Sicily because such a merger would leave the Papal States surrounded by a threatening power. Frederick also had to promise to undertake a Crusade to free Jerusalem from the Saracens.

Despite his German crown, Frederick's real love was Sicily, and once he had been anointed emperor at St. Peter's in 1220, he returned to the country of his childhood and ruled it and southern Italy as a separate dominion, legally severed from the empire. Under his hand, the governing apparatus was quickly transformed. Feudalism, which had favored the nobles, was abolished, and in its place Frederick established the first modern reign of divine-right despotism. He was, by and large, a benevolent despot. He introduced direct taxation, organized a professional army loyal to the king, and set rigid controls over commerce and industry by creating government monopolies for grain trade, textile manufacture, and slaughterhouses. He appointed jurists who codified laws into the Constitutions of Melfi. (The legal system had been in disarray since the time of Justinian in the sixth century.) Frederick's laws anticipated the rise of the centralized monarchies and nation-states

Pope Gregory IX (above right) excommunicated Frederick II after the emperor delayed his departure on a Crusade in 1227. Right, a tiara of Frederick's wife, Constance of Aragon. Facing page, top left, a coin issued by Frederick II. Frederick, in an effort to antagonize the pope, ordered the capture of a Genoese fleet of papal delegates (top right), but the imprisonment of these cardinals turned public opinion against him. In 1245, Pope Innocent IV also excommunicated Frederick, despite the protests of Frederick's minister, Thaddeus of Suessa, at the Council of Lyon (below).

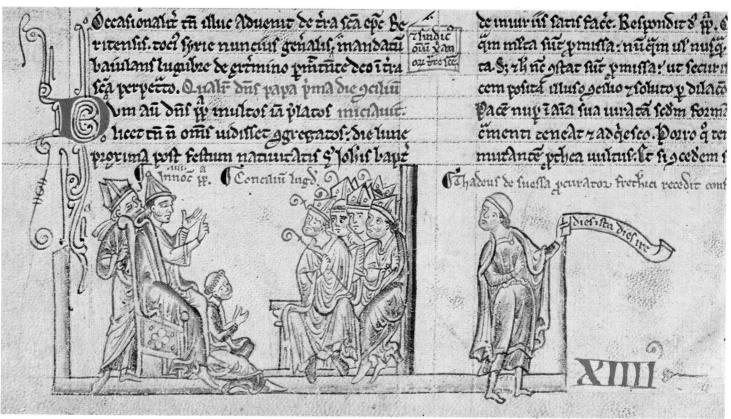

that would eventually supplant existing feudal baronies. He was, on the whole, a civilized man, who patronized science and was interested in mathematics, astronomy, and astrology. Frederick also wrote poetry and took an interest in art. In 1224, he founded the University of Naples, one of the few secular centers of learning in the Middle Ages.

The pope, meanwhile, kept urging Frederick to get on with the Crusade to the Holy Land that he had promised to undertake. In 1227, Frederick finally assembled a fleet and army at Brindisi and was about to embark when a plague struck, killing many of his soldiers. Frederick himself was desperately ill for sev-

eral months. The pope, on learning of the delay, uncharitably excommunicated him. When he recovered his strength, Frederick proceeded to the Holy Land anyway, assuming that the pope would rescind the excommunication. The pope, jealous of Frederick's growing reputation and power, chose instead to sabotage him. As Frederick led his armies to the outskirts of Jerusalem, envoys from the Vatican arrived to tell the assembled soldiers that all Christians were forbidden to serve under Frederick. Much as the pope wanted Jerusalem back, he sought the destruction of his rival even more.

Robbed of an army, Frederick was still able to

Frederick II created a highly efficient, centralized government in Sicily and southern Italy. He did this in part by constructing a network of castles that still dominate the southern Italian countryside. In the bell tower at Melfi (left), Frederick dictated his Constitutions, which codified the laws and set rigid controls over commerce and industry. Above, the castle of Manfredonia in Apulia.

capture Jerusalem—not by force but by tact. He entered into discussions with the Moslem commander of the city, al-Kamil, and startled him with his thorough knowledge of Islamic literature, science, and philosophy. Al-Kamil was charmed by this literate foreign crusader who spoke so well in the Prophet's tongue. He graciously permitted Frederick to crown himself king of Jerusalem. Frederick's sacrilegious colloquy with the Saracen foe outraged his Christian followers, and when the emperor was boarding his ship at Acre for the voyage home, the Christian populace surrounded him and threw filth at him.

Christians back home were equally outraged, sus-

pecting that the emperor was more a friend to the Saracens than to the Christians. Frederick admittedly had fallen under a degree of Eastern influence. Like his Saracen friends, he maintained a harem at his palace. His troop of personal bodyguards was composed exclusively of Moslems, since Frederick reasoned that these troops could be counted on to be loyal in the face of papal interdictions.

Was this medieval ruler in fact an atheist? We simply don't know. We can only say for certain that he was, for his time, a uniquely knowledgeable student of comparative religion. But many of his contemporaries were convinced that he scorned all faiths. He

Accused by his enemies of being an infidel, Frederick did little to dispel the charge: He maintained a harem in his own palace and chose Saracens, who were free to ignore papal interdictions, to act as his personal bodyguards. Frederick quartered his loyal Saracen troops in the fortress of Lucera (immediately above). Top, the Romanesque-Gothic Castel del Monte in Apulia. This octagonal structure was built atop a thousand-foot hill because of the emperor's passion for falconry. It was Frederick's favorite residence. Above right, the throne room of the castle of Gioia del Colle.

was widely rumored to have once referred to Moses, Jesus, and Mohammed as "three conjurers" who had deceived their followers for their own selfish ends. Perhaps his deepest faith rested in the idea of the empire itself, which he saw as the universal instrument of God's order on earth. As for the Church, Frederick thought it should renounce all its wealth and political power and return to the poverty and saintliness of its early Christian beginnings.

The last twenty years of Frederick's rule were filled with strife. When Frederick tried to extend his Sicilian regime over northern Italy as well, the independent city-states naturally rebelled. Even Frederick's

Crusades

In 1095, after the Seljuk Turks swept across Asia Minor, threatening Byzantium and committing atrocities against Christian pilgrims to Jerusalem, Pope Urban II called on the warring nobles of Europe to unite under the Church's banner and set out on a holy war against Islam. "Undertake this journey for the remission of your sins, with the assurance of imperishable glory of the kingdom of Heaven," he told a group of Frankish aristocrats at Clermont-Ferrand. "God wills it!" the Frankish warriors were said to have replied, and within a year thousands of Europeans had embarked on the First Crusade. Three years later, the Crusaders captured Jerusalem itself, plundered the city, and murdered its inhabitants. However, Jerusalem proved easier to capture than to hold. The Moslems retook the city again and again, and over the next three hundred years, more than eight Crusades would be undertaken. The Crusades served many purposes: They strengthened the power and prestige of the Church, stimulated trade, exposed Europeans to the more sophisticated Arabic culture, encouraged chivalry, and provided ripe opportunities for plunder. Indeed, the crusading zeal may have brought out the three most resolute characteristics of medieval man: Christian idealism, the zest for battle, and economic greed.

A ship (above) takes on provisions before leaving for the East on a Crusade. The rising merchant class, particularly in the Italian seaports, thrived by supplying the expeditions to the Holy Land. The leader of the Sixth Crusade, the emperor Frederick II, spoke fluent Arabic. In 1229, he was able to recapture Jerusalem by negotiating directly with al-Kamil (right), the city's Moslem commander.

Left, a relief depicting Seljuk warriors, whose atrocities against Christian pilgrims provided the rationale for the First Crusade. The enormous Krak des Chevaliers (below) was built around 1200 to guard the Syrian coast near Tripoli.

The sack of Jerusalem (top), the climax of the First Crusade, was a large-scale, bloody undertaking. "If you had been there, you would have seen our feet colored to our ankles with the blood of the slain," one participant wrote afterward. The expedition was led by a group of nobles that included Godfrey of Bouillon (immediately above).

The ultimate aim of the First Crusade was the recapture of the church of the Holy Sepulcher (right), which stood in Jerusalem on the supposed site of Jesus' tomb. Later expeditions had baser goals. The Fourth Crusade, which some modern historians have dubbed "the businessmen's crusade," ignored the Moslem presence in Palestine and turned against the Byzantine Christians in Constantinople, reaping vast profits.

Pope Innocent IV, fearful of the invading armies of his imperial enemy, Frederick II, fled from Rome to address the Council of Lyon (left), which condemned, excommunicated, and deposed the emperor. A rival emperor was elected to replace Frederick, and the pope called on loyal Christians everywhere to mount a new Crusade that would rid the empire of the ungodly "antichrist."

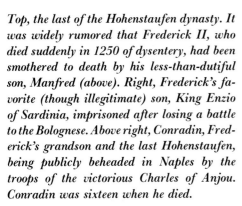

Top, the last of the Hohenstaufen dynasty. It was widely rumored that Frederick II, who died suddenly in 1250 of dysentery, had been smothered to death by his less-than-dutiful son, Manfred (above). Right, Frederick's favorite (though illegitimate) son, King Enzio of Sardinia, imprisoned after losing a battle to the Bolognese. Above right, Conradin, Frederick's grandson and the last Hohenstaufen, being publicly beheaded in Naples by the troops of the victorious Charles of Anjou. Conradin was sixteen when he died.

son, Henry, was persuaded to join the coalition against the emperor. (Henry died as his father's prisoner in 1242.) The pope, siding with the independent cities, proclaimed an all-out holy war against the blasphemous antichrist. Welfs (who supported the pope) and Ghibellines (who supported the emperor) battled everywhere. No one was immune from the controversy. Lords and peasants, priests and laymen alike were forced to choose sides and take a stand. Even the mendicant orders of begging monks took up arms.

For a while, the war went Frederick's way. He invaded the Papal States and besieged Rome. He defeated a Genoese fleet that was carrying more than a hundred high-ranking Church officials to a papal council in Rome and imprisoned these cardinals and bishops in Apulia. Their capture hurt his cause, for it turned public opinion against him. In 1244, Pope Innocent IV, who seemed on the verge of capitulation fled Rome and convened a council in Lyon, which formally deposed Frederick. In 1249, Frederick suffered a greater loss: His favorite son, King Enzio of Sardinia, was captured at the battle of Fossalto by the Bolognese, who imprisoned him for the rest of his life.

A year later, while at the Castel Fiorentino in Apulia, Frederick died suddenly. (Rumor had it that his son Manfred had crept to his bedside and smothered him to death with a pillow.) The pope's elation over the demise of the antichrist was unbounded. "Let the heavens rejoice," he declared. "Let the earth be filled with gladness."

Frederick had failed to restore permanently the greatness and vastness of the empire. Unlike the Capetian monarchs in France, who had enlisted the support of the middle class against the barons, Frederick, because of his wars against the pope, had been compelled to rely increasingly on the support of the German nobles. To insure that support, he had been forced to grant them more and more power and independence that could only weaken the imperial power.

Although his son, Conrad IV, and grandson, Conradin, made feeble attempts to reclaim southern Italy and Sicily, their efforts failed. Conradin, the last legitimate heir of the Hohenstaufens, was never crowned emperor. He was defeated by the French king, Charles of Anjou, in 1268. Charles had him publicly beheaded in Naples and proceeded to rule Frederick's beloved southern kingdom in his own name. Sicily had passed into the hands of the French and was lost to the empire forever. Only Germany, which was little more than a feudal patchwork of petty tyrannies, remained a part of the empire. Henceforth, France, not Germany, would control the destiny of Europe.

Frederick II's court

Frederick II's lively and precocious intellect astounded his masters. He is said to have learned to read and write at four, and at fourteen he was steeped in philosophy, history, theology, and astronomy. He was profoundly learned in mathematics, the natural sciences, and music, and he knew seven languages. Frederick was exposed to many cultures and traditions. He grew up in Palermo, which was a thriving cosmopolitan center. Frederick chose to rule the empire from Sicily rather than Germany as his forefathers had done. He created a diversified, brilliant, and sophisticated court, with himself at the center. His cultural and intellectual reputation earned him the title of *stupor mundi,* "the wonder of the universe." Around him he assembled the best of the cultural world—Christian and Islamic. He invited the Provençal troubadours Folquet de Romans, Aimeric de Peguilhan, and Sordello da Goito. Many Sicilian poets also came to Frederick's court, among them Jacopo da Lentini and Guido delle Colonne. The Italian language made its first literary appearance under the emperor's aegis. Frederick himself was a good poet, an excellent conversationalist, and an expert in aristocratic arms. His treatise on falconry and birds, *Tractatus de arte venandi cum avibus,* was one of the most famous tracts of the Middle Ages, and it is viewed today as the first modern work of ornithology. The illustration (above) shows court musicians of the period.

Many historians have wondered why the empire wasn't allowed to expire quietly after Frederick. Its original function—the unification of Europe under a single Christian rule—was clearly out of the question. For all intents and purposes, the empire *had* died. No emperor was chosen to succeed Conrad IV, and for nearly twenty years, as various claimants failed to achieve the throne, Italy and Germany were thrown into chaos.

Eventually, however, Pope Gregory X, whose predecessors had done so much to weaken the empire, began to fear the growing power of the French king who ruled Sicily. Gregory decided to revive the empire so that it could serve as a geopolitical counterweight to the French. In 1272, he proposed that the fifty-five-year-old Count Rudolph of Hapsburg be named emperor. He was elected king in 1273 and crowned at Aachen that same year. Rudolph tried to reunite the fragmented German kingdom, but his path was blocked by the Bohemian king Ottocar II, who had taken advantage of the empire's comatose

When Rudolph I of Hapsburg attempted to reclaim some lost imperial territories, King Ottocar II of Bohemia stood in his way. Rudolph defeated him in the battle of Marchfeld in 1278. Above, Ottocar's tomb. The center of Ottocar's kingdom was the magnificent Hradčany Castle (left) in Prague, which eventually became an imperial capital. Below, Ottocar's seal.

condition to expand his own kingdom all the way to the Adriatic. The center of Ottocar's kingdom was the magnificent fortress of Hradčany in Prague. Rudolph and Ottocar went to war, and the outcome was decided in 1278 at the battle of Marchfeld in lower Austria. In the middle of the battle, Ottocar's own nobles deserted him. The Bohemian king, choosing not to retreat but to throw himself into the enemy's ranks, died in hand-to-hand combat.

Rudolph, as a result of his victory, acquired Austria and the other territories that came to be the central core of the great Hapsburg dominion. (The Hapsburgs would rule Austria from 1282 to 1918.) To help maintain his family's control over the conquered areas, Rudolph forced Ottocar's heir, Wenceslaus, to marry one of his daughters. Another daughter was dispatched to the elector of Saxony. Like centuries of Hapsburgs after him, Rudolph happily regarded his children as bargaining chips. He was less interested in the empire as a whole than in enlarging his own family's personal holdings.

Top, Rudolph of Hapsburg, from a stained-glass window of the cathedral of St. Stephen in Vienna. Rudolph, the first of the Hapsburg emperors, acquired Austria and other lands as a result of military victory, but it was his talent as a matchmaker for his daughters that really enlarged the empire. The Hapsburg family castle in Switzerland (immediately above), only a part of which still stands, was built around 1020 by one of the earliest recorded Hapsburg ancestors. Right, a document bearing the seal of Rudolph, in which the emperor bequeaths parts of Austria to his sons.

The pope may have given Rudolph the imperial crown, but the German nobles had the real power. Henceforth, most emperors would be chosen for their weaknesses rather than their strengths. Both the pope and the German barons and prelates who elected the emperor wanted a puppet, not a leader. Not surprisingly, Rudolph's successors accomplished little. Adolph of Nassau (1292–1298) was killed by the army of the Hapsburg Albert I, who took his victim's throne. Albert I was in turn assassinated in 1308 by a disgruntled nephew who felt that he had been cheated out of his share of a family inheritance.

Despite the desperate efforts of the Hapsburg clan, the crown passed next to a rival family, the Luxemburgs. Henry VII (1308–1313) even managed to muster an army and invade Italy. For a while, his prospects for the reconquest seemed glorious. The greatest poet of the age, Dante, came to Milan and threw himself at the German king's feet. "Time shall proclaim his vast munificence," Dante wrote in the *Divine Comedy*. Dante (a member of the Guelph party, the Italian counterpart of the Welfs) saw in Henry the last hope of overthrowing the tyranny of the pope, and he begged the citizens of his native Florence to open the city's gates to Henry. The people of Florence refused and sent Dante himself into exile for good measure. Henry was crowned emperor in 1312, but when he died suddenly of a fever not long afterward, the Italian campaign died with him. According to Dante, a special chair had been reserved for Henry in Paradise.

Although Henry's death was a blow to the empire, ironically, the papacy was also in disarray. In 1305, a French archbishop had become Pope Clement V. Four years later, he had uprooted the Holy See and moved it to Avignon. The popes remained in France for nearly seventy years, a period known as the Babylonian captivity, for the Avignon popes were regarded as puppets of the rising French monarchy. In 1378, Gregory XI brought the papacy back to Rome, but for the next forty years—a period known as the Great Schism—papal succession was clouded by total disorder. This was a period in which two or three rival popes would simultaneously claim to be the true pope.

Meanwhile, in Germany, a new ruler had to be chosen again. Traditionally, the all-powerful Diet of Electors, which consisted of seven dukes and archbishops, made the choice. The candidate they selected would receive the title "King of the Romans," and with title in hand, the designate would travel to the pope, who alone had the power to crown him Holy Roman emperor. The problem with this system was that there was often no general agreement as to

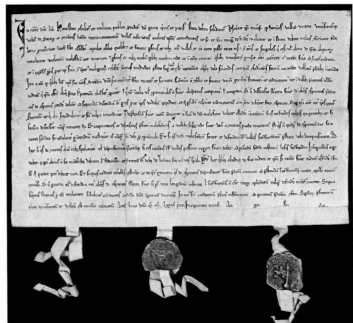

Rudolph's designs for expanding the empire didn't please the annexed Swiss cantons of Schwyz, Uri, and Unterwalden. On August 1, 1291, just seventeen days after Rudolph's death, the three cantons signed the Pact of Rutli (left), which founded the Eternal League and established Swiss independence.

who the seven electors should be.

When news of Henry VII's death reached Germany, two separate factions of electors chose rival kings—Frederick of Austria (a Hapsburg) and Ludwig IV of Bavaria (a Wittelsbach). Both appealed to Pope John XXII at Avignon. The pope agreed to recognize both of them, but only as kings, not as emperors. In the absence of a designated emperor, the pope suggested that perhaps the reins of the imperial government should be handed over to him. Ludwig and Frederick ignored his recommendation and went to war with each other. Ludwig won the war and took over the actual running of the empire, allowing Frederick to remain king, only to have the Avignon pope take away his German throne.

Ludwig next went to Italy, where he not only had himself crowned emperor by the people of Rome but also created a pope of his own, "Nicholas V." After returning to Germany, he convened a meeting of electors at Rense who decreed that henceforth the pope would have no say in approving future emperors-elect. Whoever the electors chose would automatically be proclaimed emperor, regardless of the pope's attitude.

The pope wasn't out of it yet, however. In Germany, a struggle broke out between Ludwig IV and the Luxemburg rulers of Bohemia over the posses-

143

sions of the Tyrol. The Avignon pope sided with the Luxemburg faction and persuaded the German electors that the fighting could be ended only by deposing Ludwig. They agreed and chose Charles IV of Luxemburg to replace him. Ludwig had no intention of giving up the crown and prepared to continue the civil war, but he died while hunting. The crown passed to Charles IV.

The new king, who was crowned in 1346 and ruled as emperor from 1355 to 1378, was realistic enough to see that the empire Charlemagne had founded could never be recovered, so he confined his excellent administrative abilities to maintaining peace. He fostered economic prosperity by introducing new agricultural methods. The king also moved the capital to Prague, where he founded a great university. When his advisers consulted him on problems of state, Charles would amuse himself by whittling on a willow branch, seemingly paying no attention, and then announce a decision said to be "full of wisdom."

However conscientious, Charles knew there was no hope of attaining a centralized rule over the haphazard federation of cities, duchies, margraves, archbishoprics, leagues, and principalities, whose rulers and boundaries changed with the seasons. The great families and dynasties warred with each other endlessly in

The castle of Rheinfels (above) was one of the strongholds in the Aragau canton in northern Switzerland. Below, the antipope "Nicholas V," a creation of Emperor Ludwig IV, who was opposed by the Avignon pope, John XXII. Right, the fortifications at Metz. In the twelfth century, Metz became a free imperial city, one of the richest and most populous in the empire.

the efforts to enlarge their personal fiefdoms. A new merchant class had arisen in the towns and was acquiring its own degree of political control. Each town thought only of its own interests and waged economic war on neighboring towns. Merchants who were foolhardy enough to venture beyond the city walls to trade with other cities risked being set upon by roving knights whose former chivalry had degenerated into cruel banditry.

Charles decided to concentrate mainly on enlarging his own kingdom of Bohemia and enriching its culture. He was so successful at this that his people called him the father of his country. As the historian

Barbara Tuchman has written, "He himself represented the nationalist tendencies that were making his imperial title obsolete."

In 1356, Charles abrogated his imperial power even further by promulgating a series of regulations known as the Golden Bull, so called because of the imperial golden seal affixed to the documents. The bull settled for good the question of who would sit on the Diet of Electors, and it handed over to the electors many prerogatives that had previously belonged to the emperor alone. The electors were to meet once a year to enact laws, and the emperor would merely carry out their decisions. Why did Charles surrender so much

Preceding pages, the fourteenth-century bridge of Charles IV in Prague. Charles, pictured with his wife above the door of St. Catherine's Oratory in Karlstein Castle (above left) and his son, Wenceslaus (below left), moved the imperial capital to Prague, which became an important cultural center. Charles also founded the University of Prague, the oldest in central Europe. Below, frescoes on the walls of the Chapel of Our Lady in Karlstein Castle depicting scenes from the life of Charles IV. Above, the elaborate jeweled crown of Charles IV, now in the treasury of the castle.

power? In fact, he didn't. He was simply acknow-
ledging political realities that had existed for years.
The days of imperial absolutism were long past.

In his old age Charles had to pay the electors enormous bribes in order to secure the succession of his
son, Wenceslaus IV. Once paid, the electors kept their
word, and in 1378, the eighteen-year-old Wenceslaus,
a drunk, was duly elected. Like his father, he found
the Germans and their affairs tiresome. He preferred
to do his drinking in Bohemia. Although Wenceslaus
had a particularly violent temper that flared up on
occasion—almost always the wrong occasion—he was
tolerant and good-natured for the most part. He was
especially easygoing when it came to levying taxes, a
trait that endeared him to to the people of Bohemia
and infuriated the electors. In 1394, the electors had
him arrested and thrown into prison. They released
him only after he solemnly promised that he would
take no action as head of state without first consulting
them. In 1400, the electors deposed him for good
(although he kept his title of king of Bohemia) and
replaced him with the weakling Rupert II. Rupert
reigned for ten years, but few people noticed.

The real force in the empire during these years was
Wenceslaus' younger half brother, Sigismund of Luxemburg. At the age of nineteen, Sigismund had gone
to Hungary and married the king's daughter, and
soon he became king of Hungary. In 1396, he had led
an army through the Balkans to Nicopolis to fight the
Turks, who were threatening the empire from the
east. In 1410, when the emperor Rupert died, there
was, naturally, a dispute about who should succeed
him. Sigismund claimed that the empire was right-
fully his, but so did his cousin Jobst of Moravia. To
add to the confusion, Wenceslaus claimed that he was
still the lawful emperor.

An identical farce was at the same moment being
played out in Italy and France with regard to the
papacy, with "Benedict XIII" of Avignon, Gregory
XII of Rome, and "John XXIII" of Naples all claiming to be pope. The survival of the empire and the
papacy alike was in question.

The empire rallied first. Sigismund was confirmed
emperor in 1411. He immediately set about putting
the papacy back on its feet. The symbiotic depen-
dency that had bound the two institutions during five
hundred years of hatred, rivalry, and mutual need
hadn't diminished. Sigismund convened an ecclesiastical conference—the Council of Constance (1414–
1418)—to settle the matter of papal succession once
and for all. The council rejected all three claimants
and chose Martin V. Deciding to attend the council
in person, Sigismund persuaded the Bohemian here-

*In 1356, Charles IV set forth a series of doc-
uments known as the Golden Bull, named for
the imperial golden seal (above). Seven copies
exist today. The procedure for imperial succession was laid out once and for all: The
bull fixed the number of electors at seven, and
it also provided that the electors would meet
once a year to enact laws that the emperor
would be obliged to enforce.*

tic John Huss to accompany him. Huss, who had
publicly questioned the infallibility of immoral popes
and had preached that the words of the Scriptures
should take precedence over Church dogma, doubted
the wisdom of his going, but Sigismund personally
promised him safe conduct back to Bohemia even if
the cardinals ruled against him. At Constance,
though, Sigismund reneged on his promise and
handed Huss, along with his friend Jerome of Prague,
over to the Church officials. Huss was tried for heresy
and burned at the stake. He became a national hero.

Sigismund continued to rule for more than twenty
years after Huss' martyrdom, but he was never allowed to forget his betrayal. Huss' outraged followers,

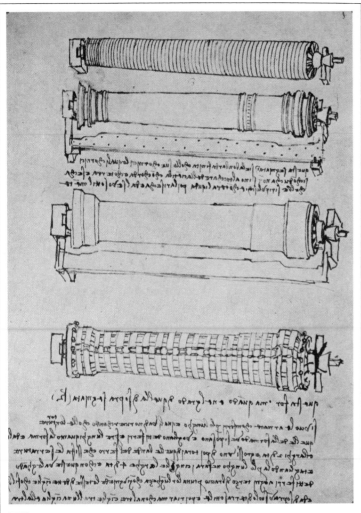

Firearms

"Important arts have been discovered against foes of the state, so that without a sword or any weapon requiring physical contact they could destroy all who offer resistance," wrote thirteenth-century Oxford scientist Roger Bacon. Bacon was referring to gunpowder, which had been used for centuries in China but was not imported to Europe until the early 1400s. Firearms eventually sounded the death knell of the feudal knight. Solid medieval castles were suddenly vulnerable to artillery. Battles were no longer decided by proud, richly attired nobles on horseback but by the common infantry. Above, drawings of firearms from the *Codex Atlanticus* of Leonardo da Vinci. Below, mortars at the battle of Grandson in 1476.

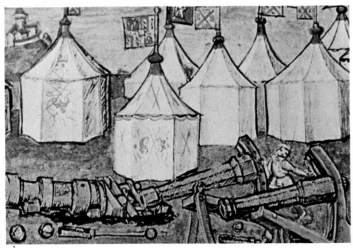

the Hussites, formed an army in Bohemia and Moravia and began a veritable holy war against Sigismund and the empire. Their cause was political as well as religious, for in his lifetime, Huss had encouraged intense nationalistic feelings in the Czechs of Bohemia. Nationalism was to be the empire's nemesis.

Sigismund's Hapsburg son-in-law, Albert II, succeeded him in 1438 and died the following year. His successor, also a Hapsburg, had better luck. Frederick III's reign lasted fifty-three years. The electors chose him because he seemed weak and easy to manipulate, and few historians have disputed their assessment. Frederick was indecisive and indolent. For him procrastination wasn't a vice but a policy. He was an immensely fat man and a heavy drinker, and crises made him lethargic. Therefore, he planned his imperial itinerary with the express purpose of avoiding crises. When revolts broke out in Austria and Hungary that urgently demanded his attention, he decided to visit Rome. There, in 1452, he married Eleanor, the daughter of the king of Portugal. Three days later he was formally anointed emperor by the pope. He was the last emperor to be crowned in Rome. "He was a useless emperor," one chronicler wrote shortly after his death, "and the nation during his long reign forgot that she had a king."

Frederick III did have his strong points. He was a generous patron of the arts when he had the funds. He was well read and was said to be an excellent late-night conversationalist. Alchemy and astrology interested him, but his main passion was the House of Hapsburg. Like most Hapsburgs, he believed that his family had a special authorization from God to rule, and he felt it only proper to put the interests of his family above those of the empire. He had all his documents and personal effects emblazoned with the initials *AEIOU,* which are generally thought to signify *Austriae est imperare orbi universo* ("it is Austria's destiny to rule the whole world"). It also meant that the office of Roman emperor belonged to the ruling house of Austria.

Frederick's only significant act as a statesman was to marry off his son Maximilian to Mary of Burgundy, the daughter of Charles the Bold. Burgundy at that time had the richest trade, industry, and agriculture in western Europe. As a center of the arts, the gallant court of Burgundy was second to none. The territory of Burgundy included most of present-day Belgium and the Netherlands as well as substantial portions of France. The cities of Ghent, Bruges, Antwerp, and Brussels now belonged to the empire. Thus, in a single stroke, the Hapsburgs became the preeminent family of Europe.

As an emperor and leader, Maximilian I, who

ruled from 1493 to 1519, was an obvious improvement over his self-absorbed father. Even Machiavelli had high praise for him: "A wise, prudent, God-fearing prince, a just ruler, a great general, brave in peril, bearing fatigue like the most hardened soldier." He was also chivalrous, charming, handsome, and well educated.

Maximilian hoped to regain Italy for the empire, but his many campaigns there ended in failure,

largely because the stingy electors refused to provide him with the necessary funds. (At times, the emperor was so poor that he couldn't pay for his dinner.) Despite his great abilities, Maximilian's hands were tied. The power of the emperor had been so reduced over the centuries that there was little he could accomplish. His only recourse was to emulate his father and resort to diplomatic marriages, which he did brilliantly. His son Philip was betrothed to Juana, the

Top, the emperor Wenceslaus IV arriving at Reims in 1398. Wenceslaus, a drunken, irresponsible son of Charles IV, was deposed by the imperial electors in 1400; eleven years later, his half brother Sigismund (left) was named emperor. Above, Frederick III of Hapsburg, who ruled for fifty-three years, and his wife, Eleanor.

151

Council of Constance

In 1414, the emperor Sigismund convened the ecumenical Council of Constance to rescue the papacy from impending dissolution. The trouble had begun in 1309, when Pope Clement V, a Frenchman who was reviled by the people of Rome, had moved the Holy See to the town of Avignon in southern France. The Curia remained in Avignon—under the thumb of the French king—for the next sixty-nine years, a period known as the Babylonian captivity. In 1378, Gregory XI brought the Curia back to Rome, but he died soon afterward, and two rival popes succeeded him. One of them ruled from Rome, the other from Avignon. During this period, known as the Great Schism, each pope claimed to be the only true vicar of Christ, and neither pope would step down. In fact, by 1414 there were *three* papal claimants— "Benedict XIII" of Avignon, Gregory XII of Rome, and "John XXIII" of Naples, an antipope who so sullied papal dignity that no true pope would adopt the name John

until 1958. The Council of Constance declared all three claimants deposed and designated a new pope, Martin V. The council attended to other business as well. The Bohemian heretic John Huss, in spite of imperial promises of safe conduct, was tried and burned at the stake along with his friend Jerome of Prague.

Facing page, above far left, the arrival of German nobles at the Council of Constance. The council attracted thirty-three cardinals, nine hundred bishops, and more than a thousand theologians. Among the council's accomplishments was the deposition of the antipope "John XXIII" (facing page, top right), whose scandalous personal life made him the least fit of the three papal claimants. Facing page, center right, the arrival of the emperor Sigismund at Constance on Christmas Eve, 1414. The trial (facing page, below far left) and execution (this page, below) of the heretic and Bohemian nationalist John Huss and his friend Jerome of Prague (this page, below right) eventu-

ally brought on the Hussite Wars. The historic council drew enormous crowds. There was much pageantry in the city, with many processions (above left) and many vendors who set up shop in the streets to sell their wares, such as snails (facing page, below right). Above right, Sigismund, and above center, Pope Martin V, who was elected by the council to replace the three existing rival popes.

daughter of Ferdinand and Isabella of Spain. While it wasn't a match that every father might wish for his son—Juana was insane—by Hapsburg criteria it was ideal. It brought Spain, Naples, Sicily, and the rich Spanish colonies of the New World into the family. Although Philip lived to be only twenty-eight, he gave the family two sons—Charles V and Ferdinand I.

Charles, who was only six when his father died in 1506, was raised in Burgundy. French, not German, was his first language. He became king of the Netherlands at fifteen, and at sixteen, when his Spanish grandfather died, he went to Spain and was proclaimed sovereign there. When his other grandfather,

the emperor Maximilian, died in 1519, Charles went to Germany and bribed the electors to choose him as emperor. He had to pay a high price because both Francis I of France and Henry VIII of England had put in bids too.

Almost at once the young emperor was forced into a conflict, the outcome of which would ultimately spell the empire's doom. A German monk named Martin Luther had publicly denied both the spiritual and temporal authority of the Church and had exalted the dignity of the German nation and proclaimed its right to have its own religion and its own church. The princes and nobles of Germany lost no

Charles V (far left) was elected emperor over his rivals, Francis I of France and Henry VIII of England. In addition to the usual imperial conflicts with popes and wars with other countries, Charles was forced to deal with the Protestant Reformation, spearheaded by a German monk named Martin Luther (top left, in a Lucas Cranach painting). Above left, Charles' signature, and above, an engraving of German cavalry.

time in rushing to his support, for they stood to gain all the Church properties in their domains. The pope excommunicated Luther and ordered the emperor to punish him.

By promising him safe conduct, Charles persuaded Luther to appear before the imperial diet at Worms in 1521, and the two argued with each other face to face. Luther's nationalism infuriated Charles. "The empire of old had not many masters but one," he told the monk, "and it is our intention to be that one." Because Luther had the support of many members of the diet, Charles was powerless to prevent the monk's escape to the castle of the elector of Saxony. Charles

Preceding page, a hunt in honor of Charles V, organized by John Frederick, the powerful elector of Saxony (painted in 1545 by Lucas Cranach, the elector's court painter). Above, the great hall of Albrechtsburg, the palatial residence of the electors of Lower Saxony. Left, the burg of Dankwarderode in Brunswick (formerly known as lower Saxony).

Emperor Maximilian I (right, in a painting by Albrecht Dürer), who was praised by Machiavelli as "a wise, prudent, God-fearing prince, a just ruler," had little power, but he was a shrewd Hapsburg matchmaker. He married his son Philip to the Spanish infanta. Maximilian II (below right), who came to power some thirty years after Maximilian I, was openly sympathetic toward the Protestants.

did manage to push through the Edict of Worms, which made outlaws of Luther and his followers, after many of the electors had returned home.

Charles could have pursued Luther even further, but he was involved in a war with Francis I of France that took up most of his attention. Charles did well in Italy, where he captured Genoa and Milan, but elsewhere the French, who had made treaties with the German Lutheran princes, had the better of it. Pope Clement VII also refused to support him, weakening him considerably. By 1555, Charles, faced with the necessity of compromising with the Protestants, was forced to agree to the Peace of Augsburg, which formally granted the German princes the right to recognize the Lutheran religion. He delegated the sad task of signing the document to his brother, Ferdinand. Charles then retired to an almost monkish life in Spain, abdicating the imperial throne in favor of Ferdinand and leaving the Hapsburg lands divided between Austria and Spain. He died in 1558.

The emperors who followed Ferdinand—Maximilian II (1564–1576) and Rudolph II (1576–1612)—only had authority over the diminishing anti-Protestant factions there. Maximilian was openly conciliatory toward the Lutherans. Rudolph, who was politically incompetent, had fits of insanity and otherwise devoted himself entirely to alchemy, astrology, and art collecting. His brother Matthias (1612–1619), who deposed him, tried to appease the leaders of a Protestant rebellion that had broken out in Bohemia. Matthias' staunchly Catholic cousin, Ferdinand II, who followed him to the throne in 1619, had grand schemes. He wanted to restore the empire to all of its old glory. The Bohemians showed what they thought of the empire by hurling two imperial envoys out a window. The event came to be called the Defenestration of Prague, and it led to the Thirty Years' War. At first, Ferdinand gained the upper hand by winning a victory against the Protestants at the Battle

Rudolph II and astronomy

Rudolph II of Hapsburg, who became emperor in 1576, suffered from long bouts of profound depression that left him unable to rule. He moved to Prague and locked himself away in his castle there to devote himself to magic, astrology, and astronomy. The greatest astronomers of the day were welcomed into Prague, where they received imperial protection from Church authorities. Nightly, the emperor studied the stars with his friends and masters, such as Tycho Brahe and Johannes Kepler. Eventually, the old emperor, whose depressions worsened and who based many of his acts of state on astrological calculations, was declared mentally unfit and removed from power in 1607.

Rudolph II (above left) was obsessed with astronomy. In 1599, he summoned the Danish astronomer Tycho Brahe (above right) to his court in Prague, where Rudolph received the astronomer standing up and bareheaded. Below left, instruments used by Copernicus, which can still be seen at the University of Cracow. Below right, an astronomical table of the period.

When Johannes Kepler (top) became Rudolph II's court astronomer, he attempted to carry on his predecessor's mission of refuting the theories of Copernicus (immediately above). After much study, however, Kepler became convinced that Copernicus had been correct.

Above, Tycho Brahe's celestial globe, which was constructed at Antwerp in 1601. Right, the palace observatory at Uranienborg, where Brahe worked with his assistant, Johannes Kepler. Brahe's main achievements were improving astronomical instruments and making exact determinations of the position of the stars and planets. When Brahe left the court at Prague, his pupil Kepler was chosen by Rudolph II to succeed him.

The Thirty Years' War

The twin specters of Protestantism and nationalism had been gathering force for more than a century when, in 1617, the arch-Catholic Ferdinand II of Hapsburg was named king of Bohemia. The following year, a group of Protestant Czech nobles, horrified by Ferdinand's plans to restore Catholic orthodoxy and imperial authority, gathered in a rump assembly at Hradčany Castle in Prague. Here, they tossed two of Ferdinand's hapless royal governors out a castle window to the ground seventy feet below. (Luckily, they landed on a manure pile and escaped unhurt.) The rebels then formally deposed Ferdinand as king of Bohemia and re-placed him with Frederick V, a rigorous Calvinist. The religious, dynastic, and territorial war that ensued continued for three decades, involving all the major countries of Europe. Because of its shifting alliances and participants, the war is usually divided by historians into distinct stages.

The Bohemian period, 1618–1625

Ferdinand, who was crowned emperor in 1619, immediately looked to his European Catholic allies for assistance in quelling the Protestant revolt. He found plenty of sup-

The Danish-Swedish period, 1625–1635

Defeated and humiliated, the rebellious Protestants eventually found a new ally—Denmark's King Christian IV. With the support of a few thousand troops from England, Christian marched on Germany. Against him Ferdinand employed one of the empire's greatest generals, the controversial Albrecht of Wallenstein. Wallenstein's army not only drove King Christian out of Germany but even overran the Danish peninsula. Having achieved another stunning military success, Ferdinand followed it with a stunning act of political plunder. The Edict of Restitution, which he promulgated in 1629, demanded that Catholic ecclesiastical holdings that had been confiscated by Protestant princes during the past seventy-five years now be handed over to him. This measure would have made the Hapsburgs the richest monarchs in Europe. France and Sweden now grew anxious. Sweden's King Gustavus II, a far abler military tactician than King Christian, declared a "holy war" and led a Swedish army into Germany, defeating Baron Tilly at Breitenfeld. Other victories followed, until at length the emperor sent Wallenstein himself to try to stop the Swedes at Lutzen in Saxony in 1632. Gustavus also won that battle, but unfortunately he was one of its casualties, and

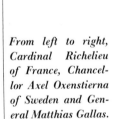

From left to right, Cardinal Richelieu of France, Chancellor Axel Oxenstierna of Sweden and General Matthias Gallas.

The Swedish-French period, 1635–1648

Catholic France under Cardinal Richelieu felt that peace with the Hapsburg empire would threaten the French state. A war that had begun as a religious conflict was becoming a struggle for European hegemony. The armies of Ferdinand's ally, Philip IV of Spain, defeated the French and threatened Paris; Austrian forces moved into Burgundy. Paris was in a panic, but Richelieu fought back partly by calling in the Swedes and the Dutch. The Swedish general Johan Banér soundly defeated the emperor's armies at Wittstock in 1636. A disastrous series of campaigns followed, led by the incompetent and

Above, Philip IV of Spain. Right, General Johan Banér at the battle of Wittestock.

Left, door with imperial seal in Hradčany Castle in Prague, where the emissaries of Ferdinand II (right) were defenestrated.

port—from the pope, from Spanish troops, and from Maximilian of Bavaria. Ferdinand also benefited from a good deal of factionalism in his enemies' ranks, for traditional Lutherans abhorred the growing number of radical Calvinists as much as they abhorred the pope himself. Lutheran

Saxony, for instance, refused to support the Czech rebels and instead took advantage of the civil turmoil to seize parts of Bohemia for itself. In November of 1620, outside Prague, the Protestant armies met the forces of Ferdinand's Catholic League, commanded by the brilliant "monk in arms," Baron Tilly. The result, known as the Battle of the White Mountain, ended after two hours of fighting in a total rout of the Bohemian rebels. Frederick fled to Holland, his brief reign over Bohemia permanently ended. (He would be known to history as frederick the Winter King.) Ferdinand then began recatholicizing the Czechs. It was a period of ruthless repression. Ferdinand confiscated the landed estates of approximately half the Bohemian nobles and redistributed them to the

Church and among prominent Catholic aristocrats. Military leaders and intellectuals alike were executed, as were many Protestant clergymen. For the moment, the power of the Hapsburgs and the empire seemed greater than it had since the days of Charles V a century before.

Right, Albrecht of Wallenstein, a mercenery imperial general who may have wished to become a monarch in his own right.

Left, the battle of Breitenfeld (1631), where Swedish troops under King Gustavus II (right) defeated the imperial forces.

Sweden's political leadership passed into the hands of the country's cautious chancellor, Axel Oxenstierna. The Swedes, defeated the following year, entered into talks with Wallenstein, who had begun acting independently of Ferdinand to negotiate in secret with both the Swedes and the French. Wallenstein's role has puzzled historians. Some think he may have wanted to become a monarch in his own right—the ruler of a new, unified Germany—rather than remain the emperor's mercenary. Ferdinand probably thought so too: Wallenstein was killed in 1634 by assassins who were afterward rewarded by the emperor. (Wallenstein has been regarded by Germans as a national hero ever since.) In 1635, the Swedes signed a treaty directly with the emperor at Prague.

drunken general Matthias Gallas, who came to be known as the "destroyer of armies"—his own. Civilians, too, suffered terribly, as the French crossed the Rhine and devastated the German countryside. Ferdinand II died in 1637 and was succeeded by Ferdinand III, who fared even worse against the French armies, in part because of two French generals, Turenne and Enghien. In 1648, Turenne clinched victory in Bavaria and Enghien routed the Spanish at Lens. This forced the emperor to sign the Peace of Westphalia, which ended the war, gave local sovereignty to German Protestant princes, recognized the independence of Holland and guaranteed that France would thereafter play the dominant role in the European balance of power.

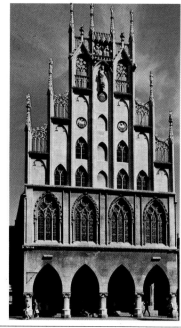

Left, Ferdinand III. Right, the town hall of Münster, where one of the treaties of the Peace of Westphalia was signed.

of the White Mountain, fought near Prague in 1620. But the war spread through all of Europe as Protestants everywhere joined the struggle against the now hated empire. The entrance of Sweden and France on the Protestant side decided the issue.

After Ferdinand's death in 1637, his son, Ferdinand III, had no choice but to face the fact that there was no hope of ever again reuniting the Catholic world. With the humiliating Treaty of Westphalia in 1648, in which the emperor formally recognized the individual sovereignty of all the territorial princes within the empire (there were more than 340 of them), the Holy Roman Empire was effectively dismantled.

The empire continued to exist in name, but it was nothing more than a loose federation of the various German princes who happened to support the Hapsburg rule of Austria. Although the Hapsburgs exercised real authority only in Austria, they continued to go through the solemn medieval charade of crowning emperor after emperor. A so-called Diet of Deputation would meet regularly to debate questions of precedence and title: Should certain envoys be seated in chairs upholstered in red cloth or green cloth? Should imperial dinners be served on gold plates or silver plates? The members of the diet were the laughing-

Preceding pages, the Battle of the White Mountain, fought near Prague on November 8, 1620. Here the Catholic troops of Ferdinand of Hapsburg defeated the Protestant nationalist armies of the king of Bohemia. Above, a meeting at Munster of the delegates of the powers engaged in the Thirty Years' War. The war ended in 1648 with the Peace of Westphalia. Facing page, signatures on the Treaty of Westphalia.

stock of Europe. The eighteenth-century Prussian leader Frederick the Great compared them to dogs in a yard baying at the moon.

In 1806, Napoleon, who thought of himself as the new Charlemagne, decided to depose the last emperor, Francis II, and incorporate the Holy Roman Empire into the "new order" he was attempting to establish throughout Europe. Even when Francis II was defeated by Napoleon at Austerlitz, he refused to hand over the by now meaningless title. Instead, he formally dissolved the empire before Napoleon could get his hands on it. It was only a gesture, but it was long overdue.

Sigillo nostro Regio Majori muniri jussimus.

Dabantur in Regia nostra Stockholmensi

die decima Decembris, Anno supra Mil,

lesimo sexcentesimum Quadragesimo quinto.

Christina

L.S.

Joannes
Oxenstierna
Comes Moræ Austriæ

Maximilianus Comes
a Lamberg

Johan. Adler Salvius

Joannes Crane

Nomine Dni Electoris Moguntini

Nicolaus Georgius Raigersperger

Nomine Domini Electoris Bavariæ

Joannes Adolphus Krebsius

Nomine Domini Electoris Saxoniæ
Joannes Leuber

Nomine Domini Electoris Brandenburgici.

Joannes Comes in Hains & Wittgenstein &c

Photography Credits

Index